LETTERS ON LIVING THE FAITH

ALSO BY C. S. LEWIS

A Grief Observed

George MacDonald: An Anthology

Mere Christianity

Miracles

The Abolition of Man

The Great Divorce

The Problem of Pain

The Screwtape Letters (with Screwtape Proposes a Toast)

The Weight of Glory

The Four Loves

Till We Have Faces

Surprised by Joy: The Shape of My Early Life

Reflections on the Psalms

Letters to Malcolm: Chiefly on Prayer

The Personal Heresy

The World's Last Night & Other Essays

Poems

The Dark Tower & Other Stories

Out of the Silent Planet

Of Other Worlds: Essays & Stories

Narrative Poems

Letters of C. S. Lewis

All My Road Before Me

The Business of Heaven: Daily Readings from C. S. Lewis

Present Concerns: Essays by C. S. Lewis

Spirits in Bondage: A Cycle of Lyrics

On Stories: And Other Essays on Literature

The Reading Life

A Preface to Paradise Lost

English Literature in the Sixteenth Century (Excluding Drama)

On Writing (And Writers)

ALSO AVAILABLE FROM HARPERCOLLINS

The Chronicles of Narnia

    The Magician's Nephew

    The Lion, the Witch, and the Wardrobe

    The Horse and His Boy

    Prince Caspian

    The Voyage of the Dawn Treader

    The Silver Chair

    The Last Battle

LETTERS ON LIVING THE FAITH

C. S. Lewis

EDITED BY DAVID C. DOWNING

HarperOne
An Imprint of HarperCollins*Publishers*

Without limiting the exclusive rights of any author, contributor or the publisher of this publication, any unauthorized use of this publication to train generative artificial intelligence (AI) technologies is expressly prohibited. HarperCollins also exercise their rights under Article 4(3) of the Digital Single Market Directive 2019/790 and expressly reserve this publication from the text and data mining exception.

LETTERS ON LIVING THE FAITH. Copyright © 2026 by C. S. Lewis Pte Ltd. *The Collected Letters of C. S. Lewis Vol I.* Copyright © 2000 by C. S. Lewis Pte Ltd. *The Collected Letters of C. S. Lewis Vol II.* Copyright © 2004 by C. S. Lewis Pte Ltd. *The Collected Letters of C. S. Lewis Vol III.* Copyright © 2006 by C. S. Lewis Pte Ltd. All rights reserved. No part of this book may be used or reproduced in any manner whatsoever without written permission except in the case of brief quotations embodied in critical articles and reviews. For information, address HarperCollins Publishers, 195 Broadway, New York, NY 10007. In Europe, HarperCollins Publishers, Macken House, 39/40 Mayor Street Upper, Dublin 1, D01 C9W8, Ireland.

HarperCollins books may be purchased for educational, business, or sales promotional use. For information, please email the Special Markets Department at SPsales@harpercollins.com.

harpercollins.com

FIRST EDITION

Designed by Jason Kayser
Envelope art © AVA ART/stock.adobe.com

Library of Congress Cataloging-in-Publication Data has been applied for.

ISBN 978-0-06-344818-6

Printed in the United States of America

25 26 27 28 29   LBC   5 4 3 2 1

CONTENTS

C. S. Lewis as a Mentor by Mail	ix
On Prayer	1
Meditations on Love	13
Letters to Spiritual Seekers	25
On Christian Formation	61
Putting Faith into Practice	79
Questions About Christian Theology and Morality	121
Questions About the Bible	159
Psychology and Spirituality	175
Letters to Roman Catholics and About Catholic Doctrines	185
Confessions About His Own Struggles	201
Questions About Narnia	213
On Sorrow and Death, Consolation and Courage	219

C. S. LEWIS AS A
MENTOR BY MAIL

LEWIS WROTE NEARLY FORTY BOOKS IN HIS LIFEtime, and one might think he would have little time left over for private correspondence. But actually Lewis's letters fill three sizable volumes of more than 3,500 pages.* Many of these letters, of course, are addressed to people Lewis knew personally. But a remarkable portion of the letters were written to complete strangers, including many Americans, who sent in questions after reading one of Lewis's books or hearing him on the radio.

In his later years, letter writing became an onerous task for Lewis. In one missive, Lewis notes that he had sent out thirty-five letters that day. In another, he confesses, a bit wearily, that he had just spent nine hours catching up on his correspondence. Yet for Lewis, responding to letters, even from children, was not just a courtesy; it was a part of his vocation as a writer. Noting to one friend that many of those who wrote him were "in great need of help and often in great misery," Lewis felt it an obligation and a form of ministry to respond to so many of those who sought his advice and counsel.

Having spent much of his early adulthood as an atheist, Lewis was especially attentive in replying to readers with theological questions. To one inquirer who asked him, "What is a soul?" Lewis responded succinctly, "I am." Then he explained further, "A soul is that which can say, 'I am.'" On the question of free will vs. determinism, Lewis agreed that it was indeed a perennial paradox. But he noted that physicists had a similar problem in trying to find models for light, which seems to behave both as a series of waves and as a stream of particles. Lewis felt that if scientists couldn't solve basic riddles about the nature of the created universe, then it was only to be expected that there would be even more perplexing questions about its Creator. On the practical level, Lewis suggested that we assume determinism for other people, that their characters are fixed beyond our power to change them, while adopting a freewill approach for ourselves, believing that we do have the power to make better choices.

Lewis also devoted a great many letters to questions that arise on individual faith journeys. To several seekers he suggested that they adopt an attitude of "cheerful curiosity," not trying to force themselves to decide whether to believe or disbelieve. To one inquirer, Lewis offered the illustration of someone rowing a boat. In order to thrust the boat forward, you have to face backward, so you can see what is behind you but not what lies before you. Therefore you have to keep your eyes on the helmsperson, as they are the one steering the boat and the one who can see what lies ahead.

Lewis's answers to his correspondents often took the form of quotable epigrams. About guilt feelings he wrote, "You can't help their knocking on the door; but you mustn't ask them in to lunch." To another reader, Lewis observed succinctly, "We should mind humiliation less if we were humbler."

As can be seen above, Lewis's mentoring letters often make use of simple metaphors and apt analogies. To someone who was worried that she didn't have the proper religious feelings to support her convictions, Lewis wrote that "faith is a matter of intellectual assent supported by obedient action, not a matter of working up devotional feelings." Noting that "we shall proceed to faith only by acting as if we had it," Lewis offers the analogy of a reluctant swimmer. Even though she may *feel* that she will go right to the bottom, she knows intellectually that the water will support her, so she should go ahead and dive in. To another correspondent, Lewis described a chronic tendency toward narcissism as a "black fire of self-imprisonment."

At times, Lewis was almost overawed by the level of trust

and devotion he found in the letters addressed to him. He cautioned one correspondent that if others read her letters to him, they might ask, "Are there no priests in this country?" He later arranged for her to have her own "official" spiritual director, an ordained clergyman. To another reader, he confided in dismay, "I am shocked to hear that your friends think of following *me*. I want them to follow Christ." On yet another occasion, he ended his letter with this important qualifier: "Remember, all this is only my guess. I'm not inspired, very far from it."

Despite these reservations, Lewis consistently answered letters for over twenty years, from the time of his first BBC broadcast in 1941 until his death in 1963. Besides addressing theological questions, Lewis's letters also offer thoughtful advice about faith and prayer, comfort to the grieving, vivid mini-parables, and even practical tips about family relations and getting along with difficult people.

One letter writer asked Lewis for some Christian books he would recommend for a friend of hers who was struggling emotionally and spiritually. Lewis wrote back that "where people can resist or ignore arguments, they may be unable to resist *lives*." He explained that his correspondent herself might have a more crucial role in her friend's spiritual healing than any other resource he might name. In his decades-long role as a "mentor by mail," Lewis himself succeeded so well as a spiritual guide not so much because of the insights and illustrations contained in his letters, but because of the character and the life of the person behind them.

---

*In referencing letters written by Lewis, this book draws from the three volumes of *The Collected Letters of C. S. Lewis*, which are abbreviated "CL 1," "CL 2," and "CL 3," followed by the page number on which the letter appears in that volume:

> **CL 1** *The Collected Letters of C. S. Lewis, Volume 1: Family Letters 1905–1931.* Ed. by Walter Hooper. London: HarperCollins, 2000.
>
> **CL 2** *The Collected Letters of C. S. Lewis, Volume 2: Books, Broadcasts, and the War, 1931–1949.* Ed. by Walter Hooper. London: HarperCollins, 2004.
>
> **CL 3** *The Collected Letters of C. S. Lewis, Volume 3: Narnia, Cambridge, and Joy, 1950–1963.* Ed. by Walter Hooper. London: HarperCollins, 2007.

On Prayer

C. S. LEWIS

Why it is easier to pray for others than for oneself

TO DOM BEDE GRIFFITHS   JANUARY 8, 1936

(Lewis's former pupil who had become a Benedictine priest)

Thank you for your prayers: you know mine too, little worth as they are. Have you found, or is it peculiar to me, that it is much easier to pray for *others* than for oneself. Doubtless because every return to one's own situation involves action: or to speak more plainly, obedience. That appears to me more and more the whole business of life, the only road to love and peace—the cross and the crown in one.

(CL 2, 177)

On patriotic presumption in prayer

TO HIS BROTHER, WARREN LEWIS   SEPTEMBER 10, 1939

In the Litany this morning* we had some extra petitions, one of which was "Prosper, oh Lord, our righteous cause." Assuming that it was the work of the Bishop or someone higher up, when I met Bleiben in the porch, I ventured to protest against the audacity of informing God that our cause was righteous—a point on which He may have His own view. . . . I hope it's quite like ours, of course: but you never know with Him.

> *Lewis refers to the Anglican service at his local parish in the week after Britain declared war on Germany, September 1939. Bleiben is the church rector.

(CL 2, 272)

Practical advice on prayer

TO RHONA BODLE   JANUARY 3, 1948

I very much doubt if I'm good enough at prayer myself to advise others. First thing in the morning and last thing at night are good times but I don't find that they are the best times for one's main prayer. I prefer sometime in the early evening, before one has got sleepy—but of course it depends on how your day is mapped out.

"Grudging," though a nuisance, need not depress us too much. It is the act of *will* (perhaps strongest where there is some disinclination to contend against) that God values, rather than the state of our emotions—the act of being what we give Him, the emotions what He gives us (usually, I think, indirectly through the state of our body, health etc., though there are direct kindlings from Him too. There are *presents*, to be given thanks for but never counted on).

Of course it is very difficult to keep God only before one for more than a few seconds. Our minds are in ruins before we bring them to Him and the rebuilding is gradual. It may help to *practice* concentration on other objects twice a week quite apart from one's prayer: i.e. sit down looking at some physical object (say, a flower) and try for a few minutes to attend exclusively to it, *quietly* (never impatiently) rejecting the train of thought and imagination which keep starting up.

(CL 2, 826)

Magic vs. miracle

TO DOM BEDE GRIFFITHS   MARCH 25, 1948

I think the *essential* difference between Magic and Miracle (leaving out the accidental difference that Magic is usually by means of evil spirits) is that Magic is held to work more or less automatically whereas Miracle is an answer to prayer. Now prayer is a species of request: and the essence of request, whether to God or to a human superior, is that it may or may not be granted, and the essence of faithful and humble Christian prayer is that the petitioner is willing that it should not be granted ("Nevertheless not as I will but as Thou wilt").

In Magic, on the other hand, I take it that the Magician expects the ceremonial to produce the result by a sort of necessity. Thus, even if there were a real "white" magic it would still be on a lower level than prayer, and not involving a personal relation and the affections but only a skill or technique. Of course the powers of Our Lord, and the possible powers of unfallen Adam, are in rather a different category from either. Magic would be the artificial and local recovery of what Adam enjoyed normally: which makes a difference. If Our Lord did His miracles *quâ* God and not *quâ* Man then the difference would be even greater. (Shakespeare's control over events in *The Tempest* is different in kind from Prospero's).

(CL 2, 841–842)

Prayer is not like medicine or magic

TO MARY VAN DEUSEN   JANUARY 5, 1951

Whether any individual Christian who attempts Faith Healing is prompted by a genuine faith and charity or by spiritual pride is, I take it, a question we cannot decide. That is between God and him. Whether the cure occurs in any given case is clearly a question for the doctors. I am speaking now of healing by some *act*, such as anointing or laying on of hands. *Praying* for the sick—i.e. praying simply, without any overt act is unquestionably right and indeed we are commanded to pray for all men. And *of course* your prayers can do real good.

Needless to say, they don't *do* it either as a medicine does or as magic is supposed to do: i.e. automatically. Prayer is Request—like asking your employer for a holiday or asking a girl to marry one. God is free to grant the request or not: and if He does you cannot prove scientifically that the thing would not have happened anyway. Just as the boss might (for all you know) have given you a holiday even if you hadn't asked. (Cynical people of my sex will tell one that if a girl has determined to marry you, married you would have been whether you asked her or not!). Thus one can't establish the efficacy of prayer by statistics as you might establish the connection between pure milk and fewer cases of tuberculosis. It remains a matter of faith and of God's personal action: it would become a matter of demonstration only if it were impersonal or mechanical.

When I say "personal" I do not mean private or individual. All our prayers are united with Christ's perpetual prayer and are part of the Church's prayer. (In praying for people one dislikes I find it very helpful to remember that one is joining in *His* prayer for them.)

(CL 3, 81–82)

The advantages of liturgical prayer in worship over spontaneous prayer

TO MARY VAN DEUSEN   APRIL 1, 1952

The advantage of a fixed form of service is that we know what is coming. *Ex tempore* public prayer has this difficulty: we don't know whether we can mentally join in it until we've heard it—it might be phony or heretical. We are therefore called upon to carry on a *critical* and a *devotional* activity at the same moment: two things hardly compatible. In a fixed form we ought to have "gone through the motions" before in our private prayers: the rigid form really sets our devotions *free*.

I also find the more rigid it is, the easier it is to keep one's thoughts from straying. Also it prevents getting too completely eaten up by whatever happens to be the preoccupation of the moment (i.e. War, an election, or what not). The *permanent* shape of Christianity shows through. I don't see how the *ex tempore* method can help becoming provincial and I think it has a great tendency to direct attention to the minister rather than to God.

(CL 3, 177–178)

Praying with words and praying without words

C. S. LEWIS

TO MARY VAN DEUSEN   OCTOBER 20, 1952

I think you are perfectly right to change your manner of prayer from time to time and I should suppose that all who pray seriously do thus change it. One's needs and capacities change and also, for creatures like us, excellent prayers may "go dead" if we use them too long. Whether one should use written prayers composed by other people, or one's own words, or wordless prayer, or in what proportion we should mix all three, seems entirely a question for each individual to answer from his own experience. I myself find prayers without words the best *when* I can manage it, but can do so only when least distracted and in the best spiritual and bodily health (or what I think *best*). But another person might find it quite otherwise.

(CL 3, 237)

The correspondent asked about "wordless prayer" in the previous letter and received this reply from Lewis:

TO MARY VAN DEUSEN   NOVEMBER 25, 1952

No, by wordless prayer I didn't mean the practice of the Presence of God. I meant the same mental act as in verbal prayer only without the words. The Practice of the Presence is a much higher activity. I don't think it matters much whether an absolutely uninterrupted recollection of God's presence for a whole lifetime is possible or not. A much more frequent and prolonged recollection than we have yet reached certainly *is* possible. Isn't that enough to work on? A child learning to walk doesn't need to know whether it will ever be able to walk 40 miles in a day: the important thing is that it *can* walk tomorrow a little further and more steadily than it did today.

As to the "state of the world" if we have time to hope and fear about it, we certainly have time to pray. I agree it *is* very hard to keep one's eyes on God amid all the daily claims and problems. I think it wise, if possible, to move one's main prayers from the last-thing-at-night position to some earlier time: give them a better chance to infiltrate one's other thoughts.

(CL 3, 253)

Praying in times of distress and times of thanksgiving

TO MRS. D. JESSUP   NOVEMBER 17, 1952

Of course you will all remain in my prayers. I think it very wrong to pray for people while they are in distress and then not to continue praying, now with thanksgiving, when they are relieved.

Many people think their prayers are never answered

because it is the answered ones that they forget. Like the others who find proof for a superstition by recording all the cases in which bad luck has followed a dinner with 13 at table and forget all the others where it hasn't. God bless you. Write freely whenever you please.

(CL 3, 252)

On prayers to legendary saints

TO MARGARET POLLARD   MAY 22, 1954

(The correspondent apparently asked what happens when someone petitions a saint who is no longer recognized by the Church.)

Non-existent saints are a problem (for you! not for humdrum little Prots like me) which I never thought of. But after all non-existent Gods, if appealed to with a good heart, probably have done quite a lot to[o]: I mean, the real God, of His infinite courtesy, readdresses the letters to Himself and they are dealt with like the rest of the mail.

(CL 3, 478)

Guidelines for prayer

TO F. MORGAN ROBERTS   JULY 31, 1954

I am certainly unfit to advise anyone else on the devotional life. My own rules are (1) To make sure that, wherever else they may be placed, the main prayers should *not* be put "last thing at night." (2) To avoid introspection in prayer—I mean not to *watch* one's own mind to see if it is in the right frame, but always to turn the attention outwards to God. (3) Never, never to try to generate an emotion by will power. (4) To pray without words when I am able, but to fall back on words when tired or otherwise below par. With renewed thanks. Perhaps *you* will sometimes pray for *me*?

(CL 3, 500)

Habits of prayer should not become rules of prayer

TO MARY WILLIS SHELBURNE   FEBRUARY 20, 1955

I don't think we ought to try to keep up our normal prayers when we are ill and overtired. I would not say this to a beginner who still has the habit to form. But you are past that stage. One mustn't make the Christian life into a punctilious system of *law*, like the Jewish [for] two reasons (1) It raises scruples when we don't keep the routine (2) It raises presumption when we do. Nothing gives one a more spuriously good conscience than keeping rules, even if there has been a total absence of all real charity and faith.

(CL 3, 567)

Prayers about other people's behavior

TO MR. BEIMER   JULY 9, 1962

Prayers invoking other people's behavior do not necessarily imply that God will infringe other people's freedom. He can suggest or encourage action without compelling them. I myself have felt a curious nagging in my mind to go and see a particular person. I believe I *could* have resisted it, but I didn't. And when I arrived on his doorstep his first words were "Oh—I was praying you might come today."

(CL 3, 1357)

Why we love inanimate nature

TO DOM BEDE GRIFFITHS   JANUARY 8, 1936

What indeed can we imagine Heaven to be but unimpeded obedience. I think this is one of the causes of our love of inanimate nature, that in it we see things which unswervingly carry out the will of their Creator, and are therefore wholly beautiful: and though their *kind* of obedience is infinitely lower than ours, yet the degree is so much more perfect that a Christian can see the reason that the Romantics had in feeling a certain holiness in the wood and water.

(CL 2, 177)

On loving one's enemies, even the Nazis

TO HIS BROTHER, WARREN LEWIS   MAY 4, 1940

Your other question about loving our enemies has been very much in my mind lately, and it must be faced, every time we say the Lord's Prayer. No exemption seems to be allowed—of [Samuel] Johnson's *Rambler* 185 (for Xmas Eve 1751) which ends thus: "Of him that hopes to be forgiven, it is indispensably required that he forgive. On this great duty eternity is suspended: and to him that refuses to practice it, the throne of mercy is inaccessible, and the Savior of the world has been born in vain." It sounds impossible. I pray every night for the people I am most tempted to hate or despise (the present list is Stalin, Hitler, Mussolini . . .) and in the effort to make this real I have had to do a good deal of thinking.

There were three words in Greek which covered most kinds of love (Eros = sexual love, Storge = family affection, Philia = friendship) but the New Testament word for "love" or "charity" is Agape, which has hardly any use in classical Greek—i.e. it is a new word for a new thing. It is obvious that it cannot mean "an involuntary sentiment." We all *say* that God is wise, and habitually argue as if He were a fool! How could He be commanding the involuntary? Agape is best seen, I think, in the words "love your neighbor as yourself," i.e. by an act of will, aim at your neighbor's good in the same way as you aim at your own.

Now you don't "love" yourself because of your own "lovable qualities." You may, in moments of vanity, attribute lovable qualities to yourself, but that is not the *cause* of your self-love but one of the *results* of it. At other moments, when you dislike yourself, you still wish for your own happiness. This attitude to one's own self is dictated by nature: towards other selves it has to be acquired.

I take it, it has nothing in the world to do with trying to pretend that the enemy is "not so bad after all" or that his sins "don't matter," or that he is really lovable. Not a bit. It's the old business about "loving the sinner and hating the sin" which becomes alive to me when I realize that this is what I do to myself all the time. In fact I provisionally define Agape as "steadily remembering that inside the Gestapo-man there is a thing which says I and Me just as you do."

If one takes seriously your suggestion that they [Nazis] are literally possessed, really it only makes this point of view easier. Suppose your eyes were opened and you could see the Gestapo man visibly fiend-ridden—a twisted and stunted human form, covered with blood and filth, with a sort of cross between a mandrill and a giant centipede *fastened* onto it? Surely you, and the human remains, become almost allies against the horror which is tormenting you both, him directly and you through him?

(CL 2, 408–409)

On being-in-love

TO DAPHNE HARWOOD   MARCH 6, 1942

My view of Being-in-love is that (like everything except God and the Devil) it is better than some things and worse than others. Thus it comes in my scale of values higher than lust, selfishness, or frigidity, but lower than charity or constancy—in fact about on a level with friendship. Like everything (except God and the Devil) it therefore is sometimes opposed to things lower than itself and—in that situation—good: sometimes to things higher than itself and in that situation—bad. Thus Being-in-love is a better motive for marriage than, say, worldly advancement: but the intention to obey God's will by entering into an indissoluble partnership in all virtue and mutual charity for the preservation of chastity and the admission of new souls to the chance of eternal life is better even than Being-in-love.

So far it is fairly plain sailing. The trouble arises when poets and others set up this thing (good in certain conditions with its own proper degree of goodness) as an absolute. Which many do. An innocent and well-intentioned emphasis on the importance of Being-in-love with one's spouse (i.e. its superiority over lust or ambition as a basis for marriage) is in fact widely twisted into the doctrine that only Being-in-love sanctifies marriage and that therefore as soon as you are tired of your spouse you get a divorce. Thus the over-praising of a finite good, the pretense that it is absolute, defeats itself and corrupts the very good it set out to exalt: and what begins by wanting to go beyond the prayer book idea of marriage ends by reducing marriage to mere concubinage. Treat "Love" as a good and you in fact make it a fiend.

As to "Fate," which I call providence—I believe that the coming together of a man and woman, like everything else (e.g. the fall of [a] sparrow) is in the hand of God. In our society the hand is usually displayed in the form of mutual "falling in love." In a society in which Our Lord spoke about "one flesh" this was not so: marriages were usually arranged by parents—and so in the vast majority of times and places. I therefore cannot make "Falling-in-love" the universal necessary pre-condition. We must always no doubt support it as against any *inferior* one, but not against *any other* one in general....

And is it Being-in-love that really makes the happy marriage work? Isn't it something different—higher? Eros won't do without Agape.

(CL 2, 510–512)

On the temptation to love people on earth more than God

TO MRS. PERCIVAL WISEMAN   MAY 26, 1942

The most helpful remark I know is Westcott's* "Only he who completely resists temptation knows its true strength"—i.e. if you give in at point X you never know how fierce it would have become an hour later. You only discover the strength of the German army by fighting it.

We are quite ignorant of the real power of our habits until we try to give them up. The *particular* temptation you mention (of loving men more than God) does certainly present difficulties. I don't expect that *was* the cardinal temptation for Him. In the Gospel accounts of the temptation in the wilderness (which, by the way, must come from His own life for they are temptations no mere human has and none could have invented) it is the temptation to work miracles—i.e. to set up His own deity in independence of His Father. You and I don't know this temptation, of course, and may be thankful we don't... or, after all, *don't we*?

The one you mention is ticklish, because is it not always *really* a way of loving humans too little? I know it sounds odd, but think it over. I mean, as soon as one tries to seek the other person's real good & freedom as opposed to the gratification of one's own affection (which often includes some will to power) isn't one driven to loving them in and for God?

*Brooke Foss Westcott, *The Epistle to the Hebrews* (1892)

(CL 2, 521–522)

Loving God and one's neighbors with more than feelings

TO EDITH GATES   MAY 23, 1944

Certainly, I cannot love my neighbor properly till I love God. As George MacDonald says in his *Unspoken Sermons*:

"And beginning to try to love his neighbor he finds that this is no more to be reached in itself than the Law was to be reached in itself. As he cannot keep the Law without first rising into the love of his neighbor, so he cannot love his neighbor without first rising higher still. The whole system of the universe works upon this principle—the driving of things upward toward the center."

On the other hand we have no power to make ourselves love God. The only way is absolute obedience to Him, total surrender. He will give us the "feeling" if He pleases. But both when He does and when He does not, we shall gradually learn that *feeling* is not the important thing. There is something in us deeper than feeling, deeper even than conscious will. It is rather *being*. When we are *quite* empty of self we shall be filled with Him, for nature abhors a vacuum. Of course it is good, as you say, to "realize" that the source of all our good feelings is God. (That is the right way to deal with pride: not to depreciate the good thing we are tempted to be proud of but to remember where it comes from). But "realization" depends on faculties that fail us when we are tired or when we try to use them too often, so we can't depend on it. It is the self you really are and not its reflection in consciousness that matters most.

May I take what is really the closest parallel? No child is begotten without pleasure. But the pleasure is not the cause of life—it is a symptom, something that happens when life is in fact being transmitted. In the same way "feeling love" is only the echo in consciousness of the real thing which lies deeper.

(CL 2, 616–617)

Natural loves are only springboards

TO MARY VAN DEUSEN   JULY 23, 1953

I take it that in every marriage natural love sooner or later, in a high or a low degree, comes up against difficulties (if only the difficulty that the original state of "being in love" dies a natural death) which force it either to turn into dislike or else to turn into Christian charity. For all our natural feelings are, not resting places, but *points d'appui* ["props"], springboards. One has to *go on from* there, or *fall back from* there. The merely human pleasure in being loved must either go bad or become the divine joy of loving.... It's all quite in the ordinary run of Christian life. See I Peter 4:12 "Think it not strange etc."*

---

*I Peter 4:12, KJV: Beloved, think it not strange concerning the fiery trial which is to try you, as though some strange thing happened unto you.

(CL 3, 351)

The advantages of growing old

TO MARY WILLIS SHELBURNE   AUGUST 1, 1953

Yes, I too think there is lots to be said for being no longer young; and I do most heartily agree that it is just as well to be past the age when one expects or desires to attract the other sex. It's natural enough in our species, as in others, that the young birds should show off their plumage—in the mating season. But the trouble in the modern world is that there's a tendency to rush all the birds on to that age as soon as possible and then keep them there as late as possible, thus losing all the real value of the *other* parts of life in a senseless, pitiful attempt to prolong what, after all, is neither its wisest, its happiest, or most innocent period. I suspect merely commercial motives are behind it all: for it is at the showing-off age that birds of both sexes have least sales-resistance!

(CL 3, 352)

The four kinds of love

TO MRS. JOHNSON   FEBRUARY 18, 1954

Of course taking in the poor illegitimate child is "charity." *Charity* means *love*. It is called *Agape* in the New Testament to distinguish it from *Eros* (sexual love), *Storge* (family affection) and *Philia* (friendship). So there are four kinds of love, all good in their proper place, but *Agape* is the best because it is the kind God has for us and is good in all circumstances. There are people I *mustn't* feel Eros towards, and people I can't feel Storge or Philia for: but I can practice Agape to God, Angels, Man and Beast, to the good and the bad, the old and the young, the far and the near.

You see Agape is all giving, not getting. Read what St. Paul says about it in First Corinthians chap. 13. Then look at a picture of Charity (or Agape) in action in St. Luke, chap. 10, verses 30–35. And then, better still, look at Matthew chap. 25. verses 31–46: from which you see that Christ counts all that you do for *this* baby exactly as if you had done it for Him when He was a baby in the manger at Bethlehem: you are in a sense sharing in the things His mother did for Him. Giving money is only *one* way of showing charity: to give time and toil is far better and (for most of us) harder. And notice, tho' it is all giving—you needn't expect any reward—how you *do* gets rewarded almost at once.

(CL 3, 428–429)

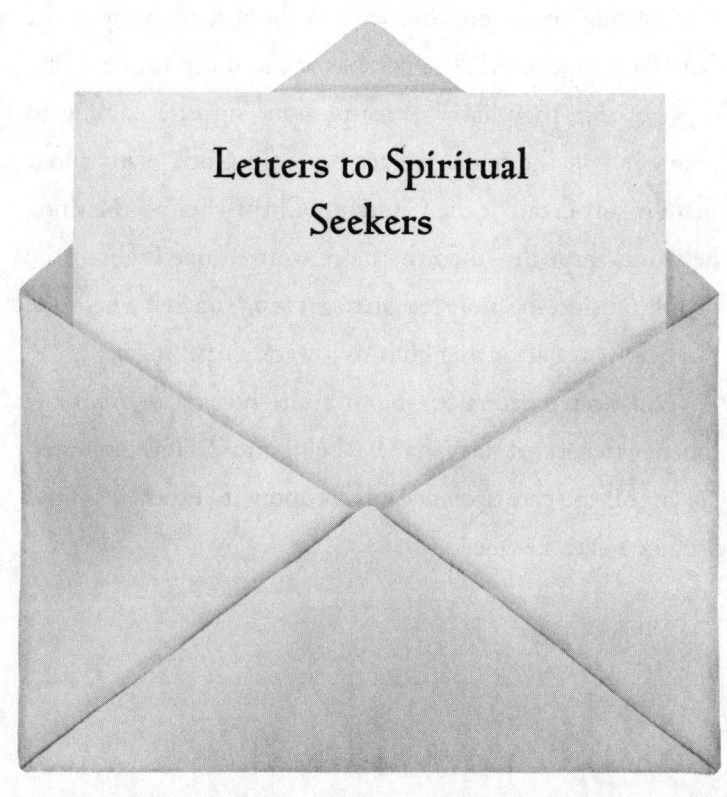
Letters to Spiritual Seekers

C. S. LEWIS

To an inquirer the day after Lewis had given a lecture on Christian faith

TO PATRICIA THOMSON   DECEMBER 8, 1941

I was saying nothing in that sermon about the destiny of the "virtuous unbeliever." The parable of the sheep & the goats* suggests that they have a very pleasant surprise coming to them. But in the main, we are not told God's plans about them in any detail. If the Church is Christ's body—the thing he works through—then the more worried one is about the people outside, the more reason to get *inside* oneself where one can help—you are giving Him, as it were, a new finger. . . .

Fear isn't repentance—but it's alright as a *beginning*—much better at that stage than *not* being afraid. How interested are you? If you care to come and talk about it I expect we could arrange a date. Let me know.

*Matthew 25:31–46

(CL 2, 499–500)

Letters to Rhona Bodle

(Lewis's letters to one inquirer, Rhona Bodle, are given in sequence here, to show how her spiritual journey was clearly reflected in the letters she received from C. S. Lewis. Bodle was a New Zealander who came to England to study. After reading Lewis's books based on his BBC broadcast talks, she wrote to him directly concerning her doubts about the divinity of Christ.)

ON APPROACHING MATTERS OF FAITH WITH CHEERFUL CURIOSITY

December 31, 1947

Dear Miss Bodle—

I think it possible that what is keeping you from belief in Christ's Divinity is your apparently strong desire to believe. If you don't think it true why do you *want* to believe it? If you *do* think it true, then you believe it already. So I would recommend less anxiety about the whole question. You believe in God and trust Him. Well, you can trust Him about this. If you go on steadily praying and attempting to obey the best light He had given you, can you not rely on Him to guide you into any further truth He wishes you to know? Or even if He leaves you all your life in doubt, can't you believe that He sees that to be the best state for you?

I *don't* mean by this that you should cease to study and make enquiries: but that you should make them not with frantic desire but with cheerful curiosity and a humble readiness to accept whatever conclusions God may lead you to. (But always, all depends on the steady attempt to obey God all the time. "He who *does* the will of the Father shall know of the doctrine").

As for books, the very best popular defense of the full Christian position I know is G. K. Chesterton *The Everlasting Man*. Mascall *The God-Man* might also help.

It is only fair to tell you that my impression is that you are in fact very much nearer to belief in Christ than you suppose: and that if you really face the opposite view tranquilly (and why be afraid of it unless you already know in your bones that the Christian view is true) you will find you don't really believe it—i.e. don't really believe that all you have got out of the books you mention is based on an illusion—which, if an allusion *at all*, must be a most blasphemous and horrible one. Conversions happen in all sorts of different ways: some sharp & catastrophic (like St. Paul, St. Augustine, or Bunyan) some very gradual and intellectual (like my own). No good predicting how God will deal with one: He has His own way with each of us. So don't worry. Continue all your efforts. You are being *steered* by Another: you've only got to row—and therefore the future journey is behind your back.

I'm pretty sure where you'll land, myself, and you will then wonder how you ever doubted it. But you needn't keep looking over your shoulder too often. Keep your eye on the Helmsman, keep your conscience bright and your brain clear and believe that you are in good hands. (No one can *make* himself believe anything and the effort does harm. Nor make himself *feel* anything, and that effort also does harm. What is under our own control is action and intellectual inquiry. Stick to that). All good wishes.

(CL 2, 823–824)

IT IS NOT YOU WHO ARE HOLDING FAST TO HIM BUT HIM TO YOU

June 22, 1948
Dear Miss Bodle

Splendid! As long as you keep in your present way—holding fast to God, whether the Incarnation can be accepted or not—you can't go wrong. Because, you see, it is not really you who are holding fast to Him but He to you: and He will bring you to wherever He wants.

I should try St. John's Gospel and the non-Pauline epistles if the first three gospels are deadened with familiarity. But why worry? (I don't mean "Why read & think?": that's obviously right). You are wondering if the Incarnation is true. Well, if it's not true God doesn't want you to believe it. If you are worried by not (or not yet) believing it, then you must in your heart of hearts believe it to be true, for who could be so worried at not believing an error!

Your own argument, that you at any rate have come to know God only through Christ is a very strong one: and I don't mind betting you will come to the Christian belief in the end. But don't read with a determination to do so. Take the books naturally as you would any other serious books. And get out of your head expressions like "theological problem," "dogma" etc. You are an adult student reading some very interesting ancient records, with God to guide you. Let them and Him work. And don't get fussed and don't demand quick returns. All is obviously going pretty well.

(CL 2, 857)

IT IS PRETTY CLEAR THAT YOU ARE BEING CONDUCTED

February 10, 1949
Dear Miss Bodle

I doubt whether I, or anyone else, needs to interfere. The route you are following at present seems to be the right one. Adding to Pascal's "if you had not found me you would not seek me" (a sentence I have long loved), the very obvious further step "And if I had not drawn you, you would not have found me," and seeing both in the light of Our Lord's words "No man cometh to me unless the Father have drawn him"—well, it is pretty clear that you are being conducted. "Follow-my-leader" is a good enough guide now. Thinking as you now do of Christ you will not be able for long to set aside the sayings which proclaim Him to be more than man ("Before Abraham was I AM"—"I AM and hereafter ye shall see the Son of Man etc."—"Thy sins are forgiven thee"—"I am the Vine")....

I quite agree that people are far too concerned about the "modern" man and this-that-and-the-other man. Why not, as you say, just *man*? You are always in my prayers.

(CL 2, 915–916)

WELCOME HOME!

June 24, 1949
Dear Miss Bodle

Welcome home! And thank you for writing to tell me: this has been a wonderful week, for I have just heard that my oldest friend* is to be baptized on Saturday.

No, one can't put these experiences into words: though all writing is a continual attempt to do so. Indeed, in a sense, one can hardly put anything into words: only the simplest colors have names, and hardly any of the smells. The simple physical pains and (still more) the pleasures can't be expressed in language. I labor the point lest the devil should hereafter try to make you believe that what was wordless was therefore vague and nebulous. But in reality it is just the clearest, the most concrete, and the most indubitable realities which escape language: not because *they* are vague but because language is. What goes easily into words is precisely the abstract—thought about "matter" (not apples or snuff) about "population" (not actual babies), and so on. Poetry I take to be the continual effort to bring language back to the actual.

God bless you: mention me sometimes in your prayers.

*Owen Barfield

(CL 2, 947)

THE INTENTION, THE OBEDIENCE IS WHAT MATTERS

November 9, 1949

Dear Miss Bodle

Congratulations. You are daily in my prayers.

Caveat—don't count on any remarkable sensations, either

at this or your first (or fifty-first) Communion. God gives these or not as He pleases. Their presence does not prove that things are especially well, nor their absence that things are wrong. The intention, the obedience, is what matters.

(CL 2, 994)

Short answers to a whole series of odd questions

TO MRS. FRANK L. JONES   FEBRUARY 7, 1950

Now for an attempt at answering *some* of your questions:

1. Why was Christ always talking over people's heads?

Since all we know of his teachings is derived from the disciples and St. Paul, we are not in a position to say that they did finally misunderstand Him. With what other account of His teaching can we check theirs? That He was *temporarily* over their heads, I agree. That is the way to get a class on, as every teacher knows.

2. About God being Truth and Justice, and nevertheless creating this world.

I'm afraid I can't add to what I said about this in the *Problem of Pain*.

3. Why did God make most people stupid?

Have you evidence that He did? Some people are stupid through their own choice—laziness, and even fear of the truth—so have made themselves stupid. Others, through bad education etc., which is the fault of other humans, not of God.

4. Neurotic.

My dictionary defines neurotic as one "having disordered nerves." This would often mean in effect that the patient, with little or no moral guilt, does as the result of his disease the same things which would imply great guilt if a person in health did them—e.g. acts of cowardice, ill temper etc. (We all make the distinction in ordinary life when we excuse someone for being peevish because he is very tired, and therefore temporarily in bad nervous health). But no doubt friends and even doctors often flatter healthy but wicked people by attributing to neurosis what is really just wickedness. There is a great temptation to excuse *oneself* on the same grounds!

5. What is a soul?

I am. (This is the only possible answer: or expanded, "A soul is that which can say I am").

(CL 3, 10)

Differing definitions of "Christian"

TO GENIA GOELZ   MARCH 18, 1952

Don't bother at all about that question of a person being "made a Christian" by baptism. It is only the usual trouble about words being used in more than one sense. Thus we might say a man "became a soldier" the moment that he joined the army. But his instructors might say six months later "I think we have made a soldier of him". Both usages are quite definable, only one wants to know which is being used in a given sentence. The Bible itself gives us one short prayer which is suitable for all who are struggling with the beliefs and doctrines. It is: "Lord I believe, help Thou my unbelief." Would something of this sort be any good?: Almighty God, who art the father of lights and who has promised by thy dear Son that all who do thy will shall know thy doctrine: give me grace so to live that by daily obedience I daily increase in faith and in the understanding of thy Holy Word, through Jesus Christ our Lord. Amen.

(CL 3, 172)

Excerpts from Letters to Sheldon Vanauken

(These letters trace Sheldon Vanauken's journey to faith, partly due to his correspondence with Lewis. When Vanauken traveled to Oxford to study, he and his wife Jean became personal friends with Lewis. The correspondence continued after Jean became gravely ill and died at the age of 40. Vanauken's memoir, which includes his friendship with Lewis, is *A Severe Mercy* (1977).)

December 14, 1950
Dear Mr. Van Awten [Vanauken],
My own position at the threshold of Christianity was exactly the opposite of yours. You wish it were true; I strongly hoped it was *not*. At least, that was my conscious wish: you may suspect that I had unconscious wishes of quite a different sort and that it was these which finally shoved me in.

True: but then I may equally suspect that under your conscious wish that it were true, there lurks a strong unconscious wish that it were not. What this works out to is that all that modern stuff about concealed wishes and wishful thinking, however useful it may be for explaining the origin of an error which you already know to be an error, is perfectly useless in deciding which of two beliefs is the error and which is the truth. For (a.) One never knows all one's wishes, (b.) In very big questions, such as this, even one's conscious wishes are nearly always engaged on both sides.

What I think one can say with certainty is this: the notion that everyone *would like* Christianity to be true, and that therefore all atheists are brave men who have accepted the defeat of all their deepest desires, is simply impudent nonsense. Do you think people like Stalin, Hitler, Haldane, Stapledon (a corking good writer, by the way) would be pleased on waking up one morning to find that they were not their own masters, that they had a Master and a Judge, that there was nothing even in the deepest recesses of their thoughts about which they could say to Him "Keep out! Private. This is *my* business?" Do you? *Rats!* Their first reaction would be (as mine was) rage and terror. And I very much doubt whether even you would find it *simply* pleasant. Isn't the truth this: that it would gratify some of our desires (ones we feel in fact pretty seldom) and outrage a great many others? So let's wash out all the wish business. It never helped anyone to solve any problem yet.

I don't agree with your picture of the history of religion—Christ, Buddha, Mohammed and others elaborating an original simplicity. I believe Buddhism to be a simplification of Hinduism and Islam to be a simplification of Christianity. Clear, lucid, transparent, simple religion (Tao *plus* a shadowy, ethical god in the background) is a late development, usually arising among highly educated people in great cities. What you really start with is ritual, myth, and mystery, the death & return of Balder or Osiris, the dances, the initiations, the sacrifices, the divine kings. Over against that are the Philosophers, Aristotle or Confucius, hardly religious at all.

The only two systems in which the mysteries and the philosophies come together are Hinduism and Christianity: there you get both Metaphysics and Cult (continuous with the primeval cults). That is why my first step was to be sure that one or the other of these had the answer. For the reality can't be one that appeals *either* only to savages *or* only to high brows. Real things aren't like that (e.g. *matter* is the first most obvious thing you meet—milk, chocolates, apples, and also the object of quantum physics).

There is no question of just a crowd of disconnected religions. The choice is between (a.) The materialist world picture: which I *can't* believe. (b.) The real archaic primitive religions: which are not moral enough. (c.) The (claimed) fulfillment of these in Hinduism. (d.) The claimed fulfillment of these in Christianity. But the weakness of Hinduism is that it *doesn't* really join the two strands. Unredeemably savage religion goes on in the village; the Hermit philosophizes in the forest: and neither really interferes with the other. It is only Christianity which compels a high brow like me to partake in a ritual blood feast, and also compels a central African convert to attempt an enlightened universal code of ethics.

Have you tried Chesterton's *The Everlasting Man*? The best popular apologetic I know.

Meanwhile, the attempt to practice the *Tao* is certainly the right line. Have you read the *Analects* of Confucius? He ends up by saying "This is the Tao. I do not know if any one has ever kept it." That's significant: one can really go direct from there to the *Epistle to the Romans*.

I don't know if any of this is the least use. Be sure to write again, or call, if you think I can be of any help.

(CL 3, 70–72)

December 23, 1950
Dear Mr. Vanauken

The contradiction "We must have faith to believe and must believe to have faith" belongs to the same class as those by which the Eleatic philosophers proved that all motion was impossible. And there are many others. You can't swim unless you can support yourself in water & you can't support yourself in water unless you can swim. Or again, in an act of volition (e.g. getting up in the morning) is the very beginning of the act itself voluntary or involuntary? If voluntary then you must have willed it, therefore you were willing already, therefore it was not really the beginning. If involuntary, then the continuation of the act (being determined by the first moment) is involuntary too. But in spite of this we *do* swim, & we *do* get out of bed.

I do not think there is a *demonstrative* proof (like Euclid) of Christianity, nor of the existence of matter, nor of the good will & honesty of my best & oldest friends. I think all three are (except perhaps the second) far more probable than the alternatives. The case for Christianity in general is well given by Chesterton; and I tried to do something in my *Broadcast Talks*.

As to *why* God doesn't make it demonstratively clear: are we sure that He is even interested in the kind of Theism which would be a compelled logical assent to a conclusive argument? Are *we* interested in it in personal matters? I demand from my friend a trust in my good faith which is *certain* without demonstrative proof. It wouldn't be confidence at all if he waited for rigorous proof. Hang it all, the very fairy tales embody the truth. Othello believed in Desdemona's innocence when it was proved: but that was too late. Lear believed in Cordelia's love when it was proved: but that was too late. "His praise is lost who stays till all commend." The magnanimity, the generosity which will trust on a reasonable probability, is required of us. But supposing one believed and was wrong after all? Why, then you would have paid the universe a compliment it doesn't deserve. Your error would even so be more interesting & important than the reality. And yet how could that be? How could an idiotic universe have produced creatures whose mere dreams are so much stronger, better, subtler than itself?

Note that life after death, which still seems to you the essential thing, was itself a *late* revelation. God trained the Hebrews for centuries to believe in Him without promising them an after-life, and, blessings on Him, he trained me in the same way for about a year. It is like the disguised prince in the fairy tale who wins the heroine's love *before* she knows he is anything more than a woodcutter. What would be a bribe if it came first had better come last.

It is quite clear from what you say that you have *conscious* wishes on both sides. And now, another point about *wishes*. A wish may lead to false beliefs, granted. But what does the existence of the wish suggest? At one time I was much impressed by Arnold's line "Nor does the being hungry prove that we have bread." But surely, tho' it doesn't prove that one particular man will *get* food, it *does* prove that there is such a thing as food? i.e. if we were a species that didn't normally eat, wasn't designed to eat, would we feel hungry?

You say the Materialist universe is "ugly." I wonder how you discovered that! If you are really a product of a materialistic universe, how is it you don't feel at home there? Do fish complain of the sea for being wet? Or if they did, would that fact itself not strongly suggest that they had not always been, or would not always be, purely aquatic creatures? Notice how we are perpetually *surprised* at Time. ("How time flies! Fancy John being grown-up & married? I can hardly believe it!") In heaven's name, why? Unless, indeed, there is something in us which is *not* temporal.

Total Humility is not in the Tao because the Tao (as such) says nothing about the Object to which it would be the right response: just as there is no law about railways in the acts of Q. Elizabeth. But from the degree of respect which the Tao demands for ancestors, parents, elders, & teachers, it is quite clear what the Tao *would* prescribe towards an object such as God.

But I think you are already in the meshes of the net! The Holy Spirit is after you. I doubt if you'll get away!

(CL 3, 74–76)

April 17, 1947
Dear Vanauken

My prayers are answered. No: a glimpse is not a vision. But to a man on a mountain road by night, a glimpse of the next three feet of road may matter more than a vision of the horizon. And there must perhaps always be just enough lack of demonstrative certainty to make free choice possible: for what could we do but accept if the faith were like the multiplication table?

There will be a counter attack on you, you know, so don't be too alarmed when it comes. The enemy will not see you vanish into God's company without an effort to reclaim you. Be busy learning to pray and (if you have made up your mind on the denominational question) get confirmed.

Blessings on you and a hundred thousand welcomes. Make use of me in any way you please: and let us pray for each other always.

(CL 3, 106)

April 22, 1953
Dear Mr. Vanauken

It was very nice to hear from you. I hope my interest in you both is something less blasphemous than that of a Creator in a creature (it would anyway be *begetting* not *creating*, see *Philemon* 10). My feeling about people in whose conversion I have been allowed to play a part is always mixed with awe and even fear: such as a boy might feel on first being allowed to fire a rifle. The disproportion between his puny finger on the trigger and the thunder and lightning which follow is alarming. And the seriousness with which the other party takes my words always raises the doubt whether I have taken them seriously enough myself. By writing the things I write, you see, one especially qualifies for being hereafter "condemned out of one's mouth." Think of me as a fellow-patient in the same hospital who, having been admitted a little earlier, could give some advice.

The semi-Christians (in dog-collars) that you speak of are a great trial. Our College chaplain is rather of that kind. I'm glad you have something better in your own church.

I feel an amused recognition when you describe those moments at which one feels "How could I—I, of all people—ever have come to believe this cock & bull story." I think they will do us no harm. Aren't they just the reverse side of one's just recognition that the truth is amazing? Our fathers were more familiar with the opposite danger of taking it all for granted: which is probably just as bad.

God bless you both: you are always in my prayers. I hope we may meet again one day.

(CL 3, 324–325)

November 23, 1954

My dear Vanauken—

It is a long time since you wrote and told me of your wife's grave illness. You asked my prayers and of course have had them: not only daily, for I never wake in the night without remembering you both before God. I have sometimes tried, by sophistical arguments, to persuade myself that your silence might somehow be interpreted as a good omen . . . but how could it?

If you can bear, will you tell me your news. If she has gone where we can feel no anxiety about her, then I must feel anxious about you. I liked you both so well: never two young people more. And to like is to fear. Whatever has happened and in whatever state you are (I have horrid pictures in my mind) all blessings on you.

(CL 3, 531)

February 10, 1955

My dear Vanauken—

I heard from your friend about 2 days ago, and today I have got your letter of Feb. 5. I am most distressed to find that my answer to your previous letter has never reached you; particularly since its miscarriage has left you in doubt whether I would have accepted the very sacred office of scattering the ashes. I would have liked to do (if you can understand) for the very reason that I would not have liked doing it, since a deep spiritual *gaucherie* makes [me] uneasy in any ceremonial act; and I would have wished in that way to be honored with a share, however tiny, in this Cross. All you told me in your previous letter and all you tell me in this moves me deeply and it is a high privilege to be admitted to such a beautiful death, an *act* which consummates (not, as so often, an event which merely stops) the earthly life. And how you reassure me when, to describe your own state, you use the simple, obvious, yet now so rare, word *sad*. Neither more nor less nor other than sad. It suggests a clean wound—much here for tears, but "nothing but good and fair."

And I am sure it is never sadness—a proper, straight natural response to loss—that does people harm, but all the other things, all the resentment, dismay, doubt and self-pity with which it is usually complicated. I feel (indeed I tried to say something about it in that lost letter) very strongly what you say about the "curious consolation" that "nothing now can mar" your joint lives. I sometimes wonder whether bereavement is not, at bottom, the easiest and least perilous of the ways in which men lose the happiness of youthful love. For I believe it must *always* be lost in some way: every merely natural love has to be crucified before it can achieve resurrection and the happy *old* couples have come through a difficult death and rebirth. But far more have missed the rebirth. Your MS, as you well say, has now gone safe to the Printer.

It is remarkable (I have experienced it), that sense that the dead person *is*. And also, I have felt, is active: can sometimes do more for you now than before—as if God gave them, as a kind of birthday present on arrival, some great blessing to the beloved they have left behind.

Be careful of your own bodily health. You must be, physically, very tired, much more tired than you know. Above all, don't yield to the feeling that such things "don't matter *now*." You must remain, as she wishes, a good *instrument* for all heavenly impulses to work on, and the body is part of the instrument.

I shall be nervous about all letters now that one (and at such a moment) has gone astray. If this reaches you, a line in answer will reassure me.

You are always in my prayers, even whenever I wake in the night. Keep me in yours.

(CL 3, 560–561)

February 20, 1955
My dear Vanauken

I was very glad to get your letter of Feb. 14. And here "luck" worked the other way. It had come unstuck and the envelope was open, but the letter inside, intact.

Your real or supposed change of luck since your conversion (whatever it may really mean) is an old story: read Jeremiah 44:15–18. And I have seen it laid down by a modern spiritual author (whose name I forget) that the experience is to be expected. You remember the vision of Our Lord that said to St. Theresa on some frightful occasion "This is how I always treat my friends." (I must not conceal her answer, "Then, Lord, it is not surprising that You have so few.")

What you say about the total Jean being apprehensible since the moment-by-moment Jean has been withdrawn (backed by the very good analogy of the novel page-by-page and the novel after you've read it) is most true and important. I see no reason why we should not regard it as what St. Paul calls an *arrabon* or earnest of the mode in which all can reveal themselves to all in heaven.*

*2 Corinthians 1:21–22

(CL 3, 565–566)

April 6, 1955
My dear Vanauken

I can't now remember what I said in my lost letter about the "Signs." My general view is that, once we have accepted an omniscient & providential God, the distinction we used to draw between the significant and the fortuitous must either break down or be restated in some very much subtler form. If an event coming about in the ordinary course of nature becomes to me the occasion of hope and faith and love or increased efforts after virtue, do we suppose that this result was unforeseen by, or is indifferent to, God? Obviously not. What we should have called its fortuitous effects must have been present to Him for all eternity. And indeed, we can't suppose God saying (as a human artist might) "That effect, though it has turned out rather well, was, I must admit, no part of my original design." Then the total act of creation, including *our own* creation (which is going on all the time) meets us, doesn't it? in every event at every moment: the act of a Person dealing with persons and knowing what He does. Thus I wouldn't now be bothered by a man who said to me "This, which you mistake for grace, is really the good functioning of your digestion." Does my digestion fall outside God's act? He made and allowed to me my colon as much as my guardian angel...

I give no advice about the thesis, and I think you ought to be guided by ordinary academic considerations. Forgive me for suggesting that the form "what Jean would have liked" could come to have its dangers. The real question is what she wills *now*; and you may be sure her will is now one with God's.... The danger is that of confusing your love for her (gradually—as the years pass) with your love for a period in your own past; and of trying to preserve the past in a way in which it can't be preserved. Death—corruption—resurrection is the true rhythm: not the pathetic, horrible practice of mummification. Sad you must be at present. You can't develop a false sense of a duty to cling to sadness if—and when, for *nature* will not preserve any psychological state forever—sadness begins to vanish? There is great good in bearing sorrow patiently: I don't know that there is any virtue in sorrow just as such. It is a Christian duty, as you know, for everyone to be as happy as he can. But you know all this already.

All love.

(CL 3, 592–593)

May 8, 1955

My dear Vanauken

Your letter is a wonderfully clear and beautiful expression of an experience often desired but not often achieved to the degree you and Jean achieved it. My reason for sending it back is my belief that if you reread it often, till you can look at it as if it were someone else's story, you will in the end think as I do (but of course far more deeply & fruitfully than I can, because it will cost you so much more) about a life so wholly (at first) devoted to US. Not only as I do, but as the whole "sense" of the human family would on their various levels...

One way or another the thing had to die. Perpetual springtime is not allowed. You were not cutting the wood of life according to the grain. There are various possible ways in which it could have died tho' both the parties went on living. You have been treated with a severe mercy. You have been brought to see (how true & how very frequent this is!) that you were jealous of God. So from *US* you have been led back to US AND GOD; it remains to go on to GOD AND US...

God bless you. Pray for me.

(CL 3, 605–606)

Advice to a new convert about not getting overly excited

TO GENIA GOELZ   MAY 15, 1952

Thanks for your letter of the 9th. All our prayers are being answered and I thank God for it. The only (possibly, not necessarily) unfavorable symptom is that you are just a trifle too excited. It is quite right that you should feel that "something terrific" has happened to you (it has) and be "all glowy." Accept these sensations with thankfulness as birthday cards from God, but remember that they are only greetings, not the real gift. I mean that it is not the sensations that are the real thing. The real thing is the gift of the Holy Spirit which can't usually be—perhaps not ever—experienced as a sensation or emotion. The sensations are merely the response of your nervous system. Don't depend on them. Otherwise when they go and you are once more emotionally flat (as you certainly will be quite soon), you might think that the real thing had gone too. But it won't. It will be there when you can't feel it. May even be operative when you can feel it least.

Don't imagine it is all "going to be an exciting adventure from now on". It won't. Excitement of whatever sort, never lasts. This is the push to start you off on your first bicycle: you'll be left to lots of dogged *pedaling* later on. And no need to feel depressed about it either. It will be good for your spiritual leg muscles. So enjoy the push while it lasts, but enjoy it as a treat, not as something normal.

Of course none of us have "any right" at the altar. You might as well talk of a non-existent person "having a right" to be created. It is not *our* right but God's free bounty. An English peer said, "I like the order of the Garter because it has no dam' nonsense about merit." Nor has Grace. And we must keep on remembering that as a cure for Pride.

Yes, pride is a perpetual nagging temptation. Keep on

knocking it on the head but don't be too worried about it. As long as one knows one is proud one is safe from the worst form of pride.

(CL 3, 191)

Short answers to a whole series of questions

TO MRS. JOHNSON   NOVEMBER 8, 1952

(Mrs. Johnson wrote Lewis to pose thirteen questions, some of them personal. For example, she asked, "Are you handsome?" to which Lewis replied, "Not that I know of: but I'm the last person who would know." Lewis patiently answered all thirteen questions; the ones included here concern theological and ethical issues of general interest.)

What would happen if I died an atheist?

We are never given any knowledge of "What would have happened if..."

What happens to Jews who are still waiting for the Messiah?

I think that every prayer which is sincerely made even to a false god or to a very imperfectly conceived true God, is accepted by the true God and that Christ saves many who do not think they know Him. For He is (dimly) present in the *good* side of the inferior teachers they follow.

In the parable of the Sheep and the Goats (Matthew 25:31 and following) those who are saved do not seem to know that they have served Christ. But of course our anxiety about unbelievers is most usefully employed when it leads us not to speculation but to earnest prayer for them and the attempt to be in our own lives such good advertisements for Christianity as will make it attractive.

Is the Bible infallible?

It is Christ Himself, not the Bible, who is the true word of God. The Bible, read in the right spirit and with the guidance of good teachers will bring us to Him. When it becomes really necessary (i.e. for our spiritual life, not for controversy or curiosity) to know whether a particular passage is rightly translated or is Myth (but of course Myth specially chosen by God from among countless Myths to carry a spiritual truth) or history, we shall no doubt be guided to the right answer. But we must not use the Bible (our fathers too often did) as a sort of Encyclopedia out of which texts (isolated from their context and not read with attention to the whole nature and purport of the books in which they occur) can be taken for use as weapons.

How can Moses preach "Thou shalt not kill" when David and Samson then slew thousands in God's name?

Kill means *murder*. I don't know Hebrew: but when Our Lord quotes this commandment he uses the Greek *phoneuseis* (murder) not *apokteinein* (kill). [Lewis uses the Greek letters found in Matthew 19:18 and John 8:37.]

If a thief killed Eileen [her daughter] *would I be wrong to want him to die?*

The question of what you would "want" is off the point. Capital punishment might be wrong though the relations of the murdered man wanted him killed: it might be right though they did not want this. The question is whether a Christian nation ought or ought not to put murderers to death: not what passions interested individuals may feel.

Is killing in self-defense all right?

There is no doubt at all that the natural impulse to "hit back" must be fought against by the Christian whenever it arises. If one I love is tortured or murdered my desire to avenge him must be given no quarter. So far as nothing but this question of retaliation comes in "turn the other cheek" *is* the Christian law. It is, however, quite another matter when the neutral, public authority (*not* the aggrieved person) may order killing of either private murderers or public enemies in mass. It is quite clear that our earliest Christian writer, St. Paul, approved of capital punishment—he says the "magistrate" bears the sword and should bear "the sword." It is recorded that the soldiers who came to St. John Baptist asking, "What should we do?" were *not* told to leave the army. When Our Lord Himself praised the Centurion He never hinted that the military profession was in itself sinful. This has been the general view of Christendom. Pacificism is a very recent and local variation. We must of course respect and tolerate Pacifists, but I think their view erroneous.

Will we recognize our loved ones in heaven?

The symbols under which Heaven is presented to us are (a) a dinner party, (b) a wedding, (c) a city, and (d) a concert. It would be grotesque to suppose that the guests or citizens or members of the choir didn't know one another. And how can love of one another be commanded in this life if it is to be cut short at death?

If Wayne didn't go to heaven I wouldn't want to either. Would his name be erased from my brain?

Whatever the answer is, I'm sure it is not that ("erased from the brain"). When I have learnt to love God better than my earthly dearest, I shall love my earthly dearest better than I do now. In so far as I learn to love my earthly dearest at the expense of God and *instead* of God, I shall be moving towards the state in which I shall not love my earthly dearest at all. When first things are put first, second things are not suppressed but increased. If you and I ever come to love God perfectly, the answer to this tormenting question will then become clear and will be far more beautiful than we could ever imagine. We can't have it now.

(CL 3, 245–247)

On being raised in a nonreligious home

TO MARY WILLIS SHELBURNE　　　SEPTEMBER 19, 1954

About the lack of religious education: of course you must be grieved, but remember how much religious education has exactly the opposite effect to that which was intended, how many hard atheists come from pious homes. May we not hope, with God's mercy, that a similarly opposite effect may be produced in her case? Parents are not Providence: their bad intentions may be frustrated as their good ones. Perhaps prayers as a secret indulgence which Father disapproves may have a charm they lacked in houses where they were commanded.

(CL 3, 507)

The "plain called Ease"

TO BETTY T. BALKE   JULY 20, 1962

You are obviously very happy and much to be congratulated at present. But don't count on its *lasting* like that. In *The Pilgrim's Progress* "the plain called Ease" lasted for only a short bit of the journey. So when you get into rougher or duller country again, you mustn't think this proves that your conversion was all imagination.

(CL 3, 1357)

On being more in Christ, less in ourselves

TO KEITH MANSHIP   SEPTEMBER 13, 1962

The whole problem of our life was neatly expressed by John the Baptist when he said (John, chap. 3, verse 30) "He must increase, but I must decrease." This you have realized. But you are expecting it to happen suddenly: and also expecting that you should be clearly aware when it does. But neither of these is usual. We are doing well enough if the slow process of being more in Christ and less in ourselves has made a decent beginning in a long life (it will be completed only in the next world). Nor can we *observe* it happening. All our reports on ourselves are unbelievable, even in worldly matters (no one really hears his own voice as others do, or sees his own face). Much more in spiritual matters. God sees us, and we don't see ourselves. And by trying too hard to do so, we only get the fidgets and become either too complacent or too much the other way.

Your question what to *do* is already answered. Go on (as you apparently are going on) doing all your duties. And, in all lawful ways, go on *enjoying* all that can be enjoyed—your friends, your music, your books. Remember we are told to "rejoice." Sometimes when you are wondering what God wants *you* to do, He really wants to *give* you something.

As to your spiritual state, try my plan. I pray "Lord, show me just so much (neither more nor less) about myself as I need for doing thy will *now*."

Don't worry. All is going quite nicely.

(CL 3, 1368–1369)

C. S. LEWIS

Should all Christians seek mystical experiences?

TO DOM BEDE GRIFFITHS   JULY 28, 1936

I have not made up my mind about Mysticism [seeking direct experiences of the presence of God].... It may be a given man's vocation to approach God mystically because he has the mystical faculty, but only in the same way as it is another man's duty to serve God by driving a plow because he is a good plowman. And if anyone tried to impose mysticism as the *norm* of Christian life I suspect he would be making the same mistake as one who said we ought all to be fishermen because some of the apostles were.

(CL 2, 201)

Good and evil are retrospective

TO DOM BEDE GRIFFITHS   MAY 25, 1944

About the past, and nothing being lost, the point is that "He who loses his life shall save it" is *totally* true, true on every level. *Everything* we crucify will rise again: *nothing* we try to hold onto will be left us.

I wrote the other day "Good and evil when they attain their full stature are retrospective. That is why, at the end of all things, the damned will say we were *always* in Hell, and the blessed we have *never* lived anywhere but in heaven." Do you agree?

(CL 2, 617)

Defining body, soul, and spirit

TO MR. LYELL   DECEMBER 6, 1944

By handing over the natural self to Christ I mean placing it under His orders and trying to will with His will. If a man does that he will usually find that one of the things Christ wills is for him to eat, drink, sleep etc. Not always, but usually. You can't tell in advance what He will tell any man to do about the natural appetites. He may tell one man to be very austere, another to be kinder to the flesh than he has been hitherto....

The natural self since the Fall consists of body, soul, and spirit all perverted and self-centered and at odds with one another. Animalness (the body and what arises from it) is not in itself bad: what is bad is the rebellious *relation* in which it now stands to the other parts. But its rebellion against spirit is less terrible than spirit's rebellion against God.

By central self or spirit I mean chiefly the Will—the ultimate choosing part. It changes itself by its own actions. By *soul* I mean chiefly the imagination and emotions. The New Testament does not use a consistent technical vocabulary. For instance in "Soul take thine ease etc."* the passage simply means "Says I to myself." I hope this is a bit clearer: but a systematic exposition would have to go far beyond the limits of a letter.

*Luke 12:19

(CL 2, 631–632)

You can keep forever only what you give up

TO PHYLLIS ELINOR SANDEMAN   JUNE 31, 1947

I think that about Houses the answer is this. Nothing rises again which has not died. The natural and possessive love for a house if it has been crucified, *if* it has become disinterested, if it has submitted to sacrifice, will rise again: i.e. the love for a house *you were willing to give up* will rise again. The willful, grasping love will not—or only rise as a horror. . . .

But the whole point is that you can *keep* forever only what you *give up*: beginning with the thing it is hardest to give up—one's self. What you grab you lose: what you offer freely and patiently to God or your neighbor, you will have.

(Your heavenly library will contain only the books you have given or lent! And the dirty thumb marks on the latter will have turned into beautiful marginal decorations—I'm joking of course, but to illustrate a serious principle).

Loving dogs more than children is a misfortune not a sin. *Acting* on that superior love for dogs—i.e. sacrificing the interests of the humans in your household to the animals—is a sin. I think myself that animals which have acquired a personality from living with us will probably be restored: but I can only repeat what I said on this point in *The Problem of Pain* (chapter on *Animal Pain*).

Remember, all this is only my guess. I'm not inspired, very far from it. All good wishes.

(CL 2, 788–789)

Don't try to create a syllabus or schedule for sanctification

TO EDWARD T. DELL   FEBRUARY 4, 1949

Everyone who accepts the teaching of St. Paul must have a belief in "sanctification." But I should, myself, be very chary of describing such operations of the Holy Ghost as "experiences" if by experiences we mean things necessarily discoverable by introspection. And I should be still more chary of mapping out a series of such experiences as an indispensable norm (or syllabus!) for all Christians. I think the ways in which God saves us are probably infinitely various and admit varying degrees of consciousness in the patient. Anything which sets him saying "Now... Stage II ought to be coming along... is this it?" I think bad and likely to lead some to presumption and others to despair. We must leave God to dress the wound and not keep on taking peeps under the bandage for ourselves.

(CL 2, 914)

The Imitation of Christ *as the formula for the Christian life*

TO EDWARD T. DELL   MAY 26, 1949

I take it that what St. Paul means by Sanctification is the process of "Christ being formed in us," the process of becoming like Christ—so that the title of the medieval book (which I hope you read) *The Imitation of Christ** is a formula for the Christian life. And no doubt sanctification would be the correction both of our congenital or original *sinfulness* and of our actual particular sins. I haven't seen that the distinction is very important, since the latter are the expression of the former.

As you know, theologians have disagreed about the extent

of our depravity. Need we know that as long as we know that it needs to be set right and are ready to submit to the cure? (The Doctor will know whether my broken leg is a simple or a compound fracture: all I've got to do is to turn up at the surgery and set my teeth).

I'm not a good enough theologian to give any note that would be safe on Rom. 8.16. You are trying to use a rough knife as a razor: I'm not qualified to give the guidance you need. These things I need to learn, not teach.

*Christian book of spiritual exercises by Ignatius of Loyola early in the fifteenth century

(CL 2, 940–941)

Mystics seek a direct experience of God, immediate as a taste or color

TO MISS BRECKENRIDGE   APRIL 19, 1951

Many religious people, I'm told, have physical symptoms like the "prickles" in the shoulder. But the best mystics set no value on that sort of thing, and do not set much on visions either. What they seek and get is, I believe, a kind of direct experience of God, immediate as a taste or color. There is no *reasoning* in it, but many would say that it is an experience of the intellect—the reason resting in its enjoyment of its object...

(CL 3, 109)

On spiritual dryness amid trials

TO MRS. D. JESSUP   NOVEMBER 13, 1952

I am very sorry to hear that your (temporal) news is so grim. Your spiritual news is perhaps better than you think. You seem to have been dealing with the dryness (or "the wall" as you well name it) in the right way. Everyone has experienced it or will. . . .

It is very important to remember that Our Lord experienced it to the full, twice—in Gethsemane when He sweated blood, and next day when he said "Why hast thou forsaken me?" We are not asked to go anywhere where he has not gone before us. The *shining* quality may come back when we least expect it, and in circumstances which would seem to an outside observer (or to ourselves) to make it most impossible. (We must not reject it, as there is an impulse to do, on the ground that we *ought*, in the conditions, to be miserable).

What is most reassuring to me, and most moving, is your sane and charitable recognition that others have as great, or worse, trials: one of those things which no one else can decently say to the sufferer but which are invaluable when he says them to himself. And of course there was no "conceit" or "selfishness" in your writing to me: are we not all "members of one another...."

You are quite right (tho' not in the way you meant) when you say I needn't "work up" sympathy with you! No, I needn't. I have had enough experiences of the crises of family life, the terrors, despondencies, hopes deferred, and wearinesses. The trouble is that things go on *so long*, isn't it? and one gets so tired of trying! No doubt it will all seem short when looked at from eternity. But I needn't preach to you. You're doing well: scoring pretty good marks! Keep on. Take it hour by hour, don't add the past and the future to the present load more than you can help. God bless you all.

(CL 3, 250–251)

How Christianity is hard <u>and</u> tender

TO MRS. JOHNSON   JULY 17, 1953

I'm very glad you've seen that Christianity is as hard as nails: i.e. hard *and* tender at the same time. It's the *blend* that does it: neither quality would be any good without the other. You needn't worry about not feeling brave. Our Lord didn't—see the scene in Gethsemane.

How thankful I am that when God became Man He did not choose to become a man of iron nerves: that would not have helped weaklings like you and me nearly so much. Especially don't *worry* (you may of course *pray*) about being brave over merely possible evils in the future. In the old battles it was usually the reserve, who had to *watch* the carnage, not the troops who were in it, whose nerve broke first. Similarly I think you in America feel much more anxiety about atomic bombs than we do: because you are further from the danger. If and when a horror turns up, you will *then* be given Grace to help you. I don't think one is usually given it in advance. "Give us our daily bread" (not an annuity for life) applies to spiritual gifts too: the little *daily* support for the *daily* trial. Life has to be taken day by day and hour by hour.

(CL 3, 347–348)

True holiness is not dull but irresistible

TO MARY WILLIS SHELBURNE   AUGUST 1, 1953

I am so glad you gave me an account of the lovely priest. How little people know who think that holiness is dull. When one meets the real thing (and perhaps, like you, I have met it only once) it is irresistible.* If even 10% of the world's population had it, would not the whole world be converted and happy before a year's end?

*Lewis is thinking of his spiritual director, Father Walter Adams.

(CL 3, 351)

The difference between intellect assent and realization

TO MRS. D. JESSUP   FEBRUARY 5, 1954

I fully agree with you about the difference between a doctrine merely accepted by the intellect and one (as Keats says) "proved in the pulses" so that [it] is solid and palpable.... About two years ago I made a similar progress from mere intellectual acceptance of, to realization of, the doctrine that our sins are forgiven. That is perhaps the most blessed thing that ever happened to me. How little they know of Christianity who think that the story *ends* with conversion: novelties we never dreamed of may await us at every turn of the road.

(CL 3, 425)

Detachment from worldly things for the sake of attachment to spiritual things

TO MARY VAN DEUSEN   MAY 20, 1954

When we speak of Detachment (from worldly interests) we meant it of course only as a preliminary for Attachment to spiritual things: as St. Paul wishes to be rid of the earthly body *only* in order to put on the heavenly (2 Corinthians 5:1–4). All the Christian demands are in the end positive—to receive, take, embrace something ("Open thy mouth wide and I will fill it")—and negative ("Love not the World") only as means to that. As one might say to a slum-child "Stop making that mud pie and come for a holiday to the sea."

(CL 3, 477)

No shadows at noon

TO WALTER HOOPER   NOVEMBER 30, 1954

We should, I believe, distrust states of mind which turn our attention upon ourselves. Even at our sins we should look no longer than is necessary to know and to repent them: and our virtues or progress (if any) are certainly a dangerous object of contemplation. When the sun is vertically above a man he casts no shadow: similarly when we have come to the Divine meridian our spiritual shadow (that is, our consciousness of self) will vanish. One will thus in a sense be almost nothing:

a room to be filled by God and our blessed fellow creatures, who in their turn are rooms we help to fill. But how far one is from this at present!

(CL 3, 535)

The presence of God vs. the <u>sense</u> of the presence of God

TO MARY WILLIS SHELBURNE **FEBRUARY 20, 1955**

And of course the presence of God is not the same as the *sense* of the presence of God. The latter may be due to imagination; the former may be attended with no "sensible consolation." The Father was not *really* absent from the Son when He said "Why hast thou forsaken me?" You see God Himself, as man, submitted to man's sense of being abandoned. The real parallel on the natural level is one which seems odd for a bachelor to write to a lady, but too illuminating not to be used. The act which engenders a child ought to be, and usually is attended by pleasure. But it is not the pleasure that produces the child. Where there is pleasure there may be sterility: where there is no pleasure the act may be fertile. And in the spiritual marriage of God and the soul it is the same. It is the actual presence, not the *sensation* of the presence, of the Holy Ghost which begets Christ in us. The *sense* of the presence is a superadded gift for which we give thanks when it comes.

(CL 3, 567)

When duty becomes pleasure

TO MARY VAN DEUSEN DECEMBER 16, 1955

Isn't duty only a second-best to keep one going until one learns to *like* the thing, and then it is a duty no more? When love fulfills the Law, Law (as such) flies out of the window.

(CL 3, 685)

On guilt feelings

TO MARY WILLIS SHELBURNE JULY 21, 1958

1. Remember what St. John says "If our heart condemn us, God is stronger than our heart."* The feeling of being, or not being, forgiven and loved, is not what matters. One must come down to brass tacks. If there is a particular sin on your conscience, repent and confess it. If there isn't, tell the despondent devil not to be silly. You can't help hearing his voice (the odious inner radio) but you must treat it merely like a buzzing in your ears or any other irrational nuisance.

2. Remember the story in the Imitation, how the Christ on the crucifix suddenly spoke to the monk who was so anxious about his salvation and said "If you knew that all was well, what would you, today, do, or stop doing?" When you have found the answer, do it or stop doing it. You see, one must always get back to the practical and definite. What the devil loves is that vague cloud of unspecified guilt feeling or unspecified virtue by which he lures us into despair or presumption. "Details, please!" is the answer.

*I John 3:20

(CL 3, 962)

How the self is like a telescope

TO EDWARD LOFSTROM SEPTEMBER 20, 1959

I think your comparison between the self and the telescope is singularly accurate. The instrument vanishes from consciousness just in so far as it is perfected. But *until* then we must attend to it; otherwise we shall be like the man who mistakes a smudge on the glass for a gigantic animal on the Moon.

(CL 3, 1089)

C. S. LEWIS

Don't become fixated on one's own failings

TO EDWARD LOFSTROM   JUNE 10, 1962

You are of course perfectly right in defining your problem (which is also mine and everyone's) as "excessive selfness." But perhaps you don't fully realize how far you have got by so defining it. All have this disease: fortunate are the minority who know they have it. To know that one is dreaming is to be already nearly awake, even if, for the present, one can't wake up fully. And you have actually got further than that. You have got beyond the illusion (very common) that to *recognize* a chasm is the same thing as building a bridge over it.

Your danger now is that of being hypnotized by the mere sight of the chasm, of constantly *looking at* this excessive selfness. The important thing now is to go steadily on acting, so far as you can—and you certainly can to some extent, however small—as if it wasn't there. You can, and I expect you daily do—behave with some degree of unselfishness. You can and do make some attempt at prayer. The continual voice which tells you that your best actions are secretly filled with subtle self-regard, and your best prayers still wholly egocentric— must for the most part be simply disregarded—as one disregards the impulse to keep on looking under the bandage to see whether the cut is healing. If you are always fidgeting with the bandage, it never will.

A text you should keep much in mind is 1 John 3:20: "If our heart condemns us God is greater than our heart." I sometimes pray "Lord give me *no more* and *no less* self-knowledge than I can at this moment make a good use of." Remember He is the artist and you are only the picture. You can't see it. So quietly submit to be painted—i.e. keep on fulfilling all the obvious duties of your station (you really know quite well enough what they are!), asking forgiveness for each failure and then leaving it alone. You are in the right way. *Walk*— don't keep on looking at it.

(CL 3, 1349–1350)

Putting Faith into Practice

C. S. LEWIS

When platitudes turn into truths

TO DOM BEDE GRIFFITHS   MAY 8, 1939

The process of living seems to consist in coming to realize truths so ancient and simple that, if stated, they sound like barren platitudes. They cannot sound otherwise to those who have not had the relevant experience: that is why there is no real teaching of such truths possible and every generation starts from scratch.

(CL 2, 258)

On the Christian view of marriage

TO MARY NEYLAN   APRIL 18, 1940

(a former student who said she felt like a "slave-wife" as a married person)

On the marriage service [in the Anglican Prayer Book]. The three "reasons" for marrying, in modern English are (a) To have children. (b) Because you are very unlikely to succeed in leading a life of total sexual abstinence, and marriage is the only innocent outlet, (c) To be in a partnership. What is there to object to in the order in which they are put?

The modern tradition is that the proper reason for marrying is the state described as "being in love." Now I have nothing to say against "being in love": but the idea that this is or ought to be the exclusive reason or that it can ever be by itself an adequate basis seems to me simply moonshine.

In the first place, many ages, many cultures, and many individuals don't experience it—and Christianity is for all men, not simply for modern Western Europeans. Secondly, it often unites most unsuitable people. Thirdly, is it not usually transitory? Doesn't the modern emphasis on "love" lead people either into divorce or into misery, because when that emotion dies down they conclude that their marriage is a "failure," though in fact they have just reached the point at which real marriage begins. Fourthly, it would be undesirable, even if it were possible, for people to be "in love" all their lives. What a world it would be if most of the people we met were perpetually in this trance!

The Prayer Book therefore begins with something universal and solid—the biological aspect. No one is going to deny that the biological end of the sexual functions is offspring. And this is, on any sane view, of more importance than the feelings of the parents. Your descendants may be alive a million years hence and may number tens of thousands. In this regard marriages are the fountains of History. Surely to put the mere emotional aspects first would be sheer sentimentalism. Then the second reason. Forgive me: but it is simply no good trying to explain this to a woman.

The emotional temptations may be worse for women than for men: but the pressure of mere appetite on the male, they simply don't understand. In this second reason, the Prayer Book is saying "If you can't be chaste (and most of you can't) the alternative is marriage." This may be brutal sense, but, to a man, it is sense, and that's that. The third reason gives the thing that matters far more than "being in love" and will last and increase, between good people, long after "love" in the popular sense is only as a memory of childhood—the partnership, the loyalty to "the firm," the composite creature. (Remember it is not a cynic but a devoted husband and inconsolable widower, Dr. Johnson, who said that a man who has been happy with one woman could have been equally happy with any one of "tens of thousands" of other women. i.e. the original attraction will turn out in the end to have been almost accidental: it is what is built up on that, or any other, basis which may have brought the people together that matters.)

Now the second reason involves the whole Christian view of sex. It is all contained in Christ's saying that two shall be "one flesh." He says nothing about two "who married for love": the mere fact of marriage at all—however it came about—sets up the "one flesh." There is a terrible comment on this in I Corinthians 6:16 "he that is joined to a harlot is one flesh." You see? Apparently, if Christianity is true, the mere fact of sexual intercourse sets up between human beings a relation which has, so to speak, transcendental repercussions—some eternal relation is established whether they like it or not.

This sounds very odd. But is it? After all, if there is an eternal world and if our world is its manifestation, then you would expect bits of it to "stick through" into ours. We are like children pulling the levers of a vast machine of which most is concealed. We see a few little wheels that buzz round on this side when we start it up—but what glorious or frightful processes we are initiating in there, we don't know. That's why it is so important to do what we're told (cf.—what does the Holy Communion imply about the real significance of eating?) . . .

(CL 2, 392–394)

On deciding to go to confession

TO SISTER PENELOPE   OCTOBER 24, 1940

I am going to make my first confession next week, which will seem odd to you, but I wasn't brought up to that kind of thing. It's an odd experience. The *decision* to do so was one of the hardest I have ever made: but now that I am committed (by dint of posting the letter before I had time to change my mind) I begin to be afraid of the opposite extreme—afraid that I am merely indulging in an orgy of egoism. However, *quod ubique quod ab omnibus!** It *will* be terrifying to face the A.T.S. [Association of Theological Schools] but it is a wonderful opportunity. Remember that resistance at the time means very little. Those who resist most violently in words are often those who go away and think it over most fruitfully.

*Reference to the Latin phrase which means "believed everywhere, by all, at all times"

(CL 2, 452)

To a correspondent who worried her questions were taking up too much of Lewis's time

TO MARY NEYLAN   APRIL 30, 1941

You may put out of your head any idea of "not having a claim" on any help I can give. Every human being, still more every Christian, has an absolute claim on me for any service I can render them without neglecting other duties.

(CL 2, 482)

Saying and doing in the Christian life

TO THE EDITOR OF *THE LISTENER* MARCH 9, 1944

It is no use to say "Lord, Lord," if we do not do what Christ tells us: that, indeed, is one of the reasons why I think an aesthetic religion of "flowers and music" insufficient. My reason for thinking that a mere statement of even the highest ethical principles is not enough is precisely that to know these things is not necessarily to do them, and if Christianity brought no healing to the impotent will, Christ's teaching would not help us.

(CL 2, 605)

To a correspondent whose friend was struggling with her faith

TO MISS GLADDING JUNE 7, 1945

I am afraid I don't know any books more elementary than my own which would help. The truth is that when a person (not herself very bookish or philosophical) has lost faith under so very great and bewildering a trial, no *intellectual* approach is likely to avail. But where people can resist and ignore arguments they may be unable to resist *lives*. I am afraid, my dear lady, the only hope lies in you and in any other Christian friends she has. It is insofar as you succeed in representing Christ to her by all your actions and words that she may, even unconsciously, come to know Him. This is a terrible thing to say to you, but He will make you able to be what you need to be.

(CL 2, 659)

Worrying about the state of the world

TO DOM BEDE GRIFFITHS   DECEMBER 20, 1946

It is one of the evils of rapid diffusion of news that the sorrows of *all* the world come to us every morning. I think each village was meant to feel pity for *its own* sick and poor whom it can help and I doubt if it is the duty of any private person to fix his mind on ills which he cannot help. (This may even become an *escape* from the works of charity we really *can* do to those we know).

A great many people (not you) do now seem to think that the mere state of being *worried* is in itself meritorious. I don't think it is. We must, if it so happens, give our lives for others: but even while we're doing it, I think we're meant to enjoy Our Lord and, in Him, our friends, our food, our sleep, our jokes, and the bird's song and the frosty sunrise.

As about the distant, so about the future. It is very dark:

but there's usually light enough for the next step or so. Pray for me always.

(CL 2, 747–748)

Ambition

TO WARFIELD M. FIROR   MARCH 12, 1950

Boys are now taught to regard *Ambition* as a virtue. I think we shall find that up to the 18th Century, and back into pagan times, all moralists regarded it as a vice and dealt with it accordingly.

(CL 3, 17)

On Public and Private Worship

TO MARY VAN DEUSEN   DECEMBER 7, 1950

The only rite which we know to have been instituted by Our Lord Himself is the Holy Communion ("Do this in remembrance of me"—"If you do not eat the flesh of the Son of man and drink His blood, ye have no life in you"). This is an order and must be obeyed. The other services are, I take it, traditional and might lawfully be altered. But the New Testament does not envisage solitary religion: some kind of regular assembly for worship and instruction is everywhere taken for granted in the Epistles. So we must be regular practicing members of the Church.

Of course we differ in temperament. Some (like you—and me) find it more natural to approach God in solitude: but we must go to church as well. Others find it easier to approach Him thro' the services: but they must practice private prayer and reading as well. For the Church is not a human society of people united by their natural affinities but the Body of Christ in which all members however different (and He rejoices in their differences and by no means wishes to iron them out) must share the common life, complementing and helping and receiving one another precisely by their differences. (Reread 1st Corinthians, chapter 12, and meditate on it. The word translated *members* would perhaps be better translated *organs*).

If people like you and me find much that we don't naturally like in the public and corporate side of Christianity all the better for us: it will teach us humility and charity towards simple lowbrow people who may be better Christians than ourselves. I naturally *loathe* nearly all hymns: the face, and life, of the charwoman in the next pew who revels in them, teach me that good taste in poetry or music are *not* necessary to salvation. . . .

"Regular but cool" in Church attendance is no bad symptom. Obedience is the key to all doors: *feelings* come (or don't come) and go as God pleases. We can't produce them at will and mustn't try.

(CL 3, 68–69)

To a recent convert whose husband was not a Christian

TO MRS. JESSUP   OCTOBER 15, 1951

Our regeneration is a slow process. As Charles Williams says there are three stages: (1.) The Old Self on the Old Way. (2.) The Old Self on the New Way. (3.) The New Self on the New Way.

After conversion the Old Self can of course be just as arrogant, importunate, and imperialistic about the Faith as it previously was about any other interest. I had almost said "Any other Fad"—for just as the loveliest complexion turns green in a green light, so the Faith itself may have at first all the characteristics of a Fad and we may be as ill to live with as if we had taken up Nudism or Psychoanalysis or Pure Wool Clothing. You and I, clearly, both know all about that: one makes blunders.

About obedience, the principle is clear. Obedience to man is limited by obedience to God and, when they really conflict, must go. But of course that gives one very little guidance about particulars. The converted party must pray: I suppose it is not often necessary to pray *in the presence* of the other! Especially if the converted party is the woman, who usually has the house to herself all day. Of course there must be no *concealment*, in the sense that if the question comes up one must say frankly that one does pray. But there is a difference between not concealing and *flaunting*. For the rest (did I quote this before?) MacDonald says "the time for *speaking* seldom arrives, the time for being never departs." Let you and me pray for each other.

(CL 3, 141)

The principle of vicariousness in the universe

TO MARY VAN DEUSEN   JUNE 10, 1952

We can *all* "take" from a stranger what we can't "take" from our own parents. I listen with profit to elderly friends saying the very same things which I neglected or even resented when my father said them. Nay more: I can obey advice from others which I have often given myself in vain. I suppose this is one aspect of the *vicariousness* of the universe: Charles Williams's view that everyone can help to paddle everyone else's canoe better than his own. We must bear one another's burdens because that is the only way the burdens can get borne: and "He saved others, himself He cannot save" is a fundamental law.

(CL 3, 200)

How to combat the prideful feeling that "I'm special"

TO GENIA GOELZ   JUNE 20, 1952

I would prefer to combat the "I'm special" feeling not by the thought "I'm no more special than anyone else" but by the feeling "Everyone is as special as me." In one way there is no difference, I grant, for both remove the specialty. But there is a difference in another way. The first might lead you to think, "I'm only one of the crowd like anyone else." But the second leads to the truth that there isn't any crowd. No one is like anyone else. All are "members" (organs) in the Body of Christ. All different and all necessary to the whole and to one another: each loved by God individually, as if it were the only creature in existence. Otherwise you might get the idea that God is like the government which can only deal with the people in the mass.

(CL 3, 204)

How the Spirit speaks

TO GENIA GOELZ   JUNE 20, 1952

About confession, I take it that the view of our Church is that everyone may use it but none is obliged to. I don't doubt that the Holy Spirit guides your decisions from within when you make them with the intention of pleasing God. The error would be to think that He speaks *only* within whereas, in reality, He speaks also through Scripture, the Church, Christian friends, books etc.

(CL 3, 204)

Dealing with religious faultfinders

TO MARY VAN DEUSEN   JUNE 26, 1952

I think we may except [accept] it as a rule that whenever a person's religious conversation dwells chiefly, or even frequently, on the faults of other people's religions, he is in a bad condition. The fact that he shakes your faith is significant. Pray *for* him but not, I should say, *with* him. If he insists on talking religion to you ask him for positive things: ask him to tell you what he knows of God.

(CL 3, 209)

Those who get lost and blame the map

TO MISS REIDY JUNE 28, 1952

The point was that as foolish people on a walk, when by their own errors they are off the course, think the map was wrong, so, when we do not find in ourselves the fruits of the Spirit which all our teachers promise, it is not that the promise was false, but that we have failed to use the Grace we have been given. The "map" can be found in almost any Christian teaching.

(CL 3, 210)

On resisting unwanted thoughts

TO VERA GEBBERT MARCH 23, 1953

One can't help momentary wishes: guilt begins only when one embraces them. You can't help their knocking at the door, but one mustn't ask them in to lunch.

(CL 3, 310)

On going to confession

TO MARY VAN DEUSEN APRIL 6, 1953

I think our [Anglican] official view of confession can be seen in the form for the Visitation of the Sick where it says "Then shall the sick person be moved (i.e. advised, prompted) to make a ... Confession ... if he feel his conscience troubled with any weighty matter." That is, where Rome makes Confession compulsory for all, we make it permissible for any: not "generally necessary" but profitable. We do not doubt that there can be forgiveness without it. But, as your own experience shows, many people do not *feel* forgiven, i.e. do not effectively "believe in the forgiveness of sins," without it. The quite enormous advantage of coming really to believe in forgiveness is well worth the horrors (I agree, they *are* horrors) of a first confession.

Also, there is the gain in self-knowledge: most of [us] have never really faced the facts about ourselves until we uttered them aloud in plain words, calling a spade a spade. I certainly feel I have profited enormously by the practice. At the same time I think we are quite right not to make it generally obligatory, which would force it on some who are not ready for it and might do harm.

As for conduct of services, surely a wide latitude is reasonable. Has not each kind—the very "low" and the very "high"—its own value? [i.e., Low Church and High Church]. ...

(CL 3, 320)

On giving advice to those who didn't ask for it

TO MARY VAN DEUSEN   APRIL 6, 1953

I think advice is best kept till it is asked for. . . . One must beware of meddling.

(CL 3, 320)

The difficulties of trying to evangelize casual acquaintances or strangers

TO MARY VAN DEUSEN   APRIL 7, 1953

About putting one's Christian point of view to doctors and other unpromising subjects I'm in great doubt myself. All I'm clear about is that one sins if one's real reasons for silence is simply the fear of looking a fool. I suppose one is right if one's reason is that the other party will be repelled still further and only confirmed in his belief that Christians are troublesome and embarrassing people, to be avoided whenever possible. But I find it a dreadfully worrying problem. (I am quite sure that an importunate bit of evangelization from a comparative stranger would *not* have done me any good when *I* was an unbeliever.)

(CL 3, 321)

C. S. LEWIS

Is there a decline in Christian faith or just in conventional churchgoing?

TO MARY WILLIS SHELBURNE   MAY 9, 1953

I am afraid it is certainly true in England that Christians are in the minority. But remember, the change from, say, thirty years ago, consists largely in the fact that nominal Christianity has died out, so that only those who really believe now profess. The old conventional church-going of semi-believers or almost total unbelievers is a thing of the past. Whether the real thing is rarer than it was would be hard to say. Fewer children are brought up to it: but adult conversions are very frequent.

(CL 3, 326)

How we blame everyone but ourselves

TO MARY WILLIS SHELBURNE   MAY 30, 1953

Yes, we are always told that the present widespread apostasy must be the fault of the clergy, not of the laity. If I were a parson I should always try to dwell on the faults of the clergy: being a layman, I think it more wholesome to concentrate on those of the laity. I am rather sick of the modern assumption that, for all events, "WE," the people, are never responsible: it is always our rulers, or ancestors, or parents, or education, or anybody but precious "US." WE are apparently perfect and blameless. Don't you believe it.

(CL 3, 333)

Religious practices as the handrail not the staircase

TO MARY VAN DEUSEN   JUNE [2]9, 1953

I wouldn't quite say that "religious Practices help the search for truth" for that might imply that they have no further use when the Truth has been found. I think about the practices what a wise old priest said to me* about a "rule of life" in general— "It is not a stair but a banister" (or rail or balustrade—I don't know what you call it in America), i.e. it is, not the thing you ascend by but it is a protective against falling off and a help-up. I think thus we ascend. The stair is God's grace. One's climb from step to step is obedience. Many different kinds of banisters exist, all legitimate. It is possible to get up without any banisters, if need be: but no one would willingly build a staircase without them because it would be less safe, more laborious, and a little lacking in beauty.

*Lewis may be referring to Walter Hilton's *The Scale of Perfection*.

(CL 3, 342)

On giving advice and listening to advice

TO MARY VAN DEUSEN   OCTOBER 3, 1953

If few can give good advice, fewer still can hear with patience advice either good or bad.

(CL 3, 369)

To a correspondent who was dissatisfied with her parish priest

TO MARY VAN DEUSEN   DECEMBER 28, 1953

I think someone ought to write a book on "Christian life for Laymen under a bad Parish Priest" for the problem is bound to occur in the best churches. The motto would be of course Herbert's lines about the sermon "If all lack sense, God takes a text and preaches patience."

(CL 3, 397)

Pride as a kind of itch

TO MRS. JOHNSON   FEBRUARY 18, 1954

Yes, I know one doesn't even *want* to be cured of one's pride because it gives pleasure. But the pleasure of pride is like the pleasure of scratching. If there is an itch one does want to scratch: but it is much nicer to have *neither* the itch *nor* the scratch. As long as we have the itch of self-regard we shall want the pleasure of self-approval: but the happiest moments are those when we forget our precious selves and have neither but have everything else (God, our fellow humans, animals, the garden and the sky) instead.

(CL 3, 429)

On combating fears

TO MARY VAN DEUSEN   FEBRUARY 22, 1954

If only people (including myself: I also have fears) were still brought up with the idea that life is a battle where death and wounds await us at every moment, so that courage is the first and most necessary of virtues, things would be easier. As it is, fears are all the harder to combat because they disappoint expectations bred on modern poppycock in which unbroken security is regarded as somehow "normal" and the touch of reality as anomalous. Notice, too, how our bad habit of lying to those who are really ill renders vain our true assurances to those who are not!

(CL 3, 432)

On dealing with nasty people

TO MARY WILLIS SHELBURNE   MARCH 10, 1954

I am very puzzled by people like your Committee Secretary, people who are just nasty. I find it easier to understand the great crimes, for the raw material of them exists in us all; the mere disagreeableness which seems to spring from no recognizable passion is mysterious. (Like the total stranger in a train of whom I once asked "Do you know when we get to Liverpool" and who replied "I'm not paid to answer your questions: ask the guard"). I have found it more among Boys than anyone else. That makes me think it really comes from inner insecurity—a dim sense that one is Nobody, a strong determination to be Somebody, and a belief that this can be achieved by arrogance. Probably *you*, who can't hit back, come in for a good deal of *resentful* arrogance aroused by others on whom she doesn't vent it, because they *can*. (A bully in an Elizabethan play, having been sat on by a man he dare not fight, says "I'll go home and beat all my servants"). But I mustn't encourage you to go on thinking about her: that, after all, is almost the greatest evil nasty people can do us—to become an obsession, to haunt our minds. A brief prayer for them, and then away to other subjects, is the thing, if one can only stick to it.

(CL 3, 438)

A parable about fear

TO MRS. D. JESSUP MARCH 26, 1954

One last word, about getting rid of fear.

Two men had to cross a dangerous bridge. The first convinced himself that it would bear them, and called this conviction Faith. The second said "Whether it breaks or holds, whether I die here or somewhere else, I am equally in God's good hands." And the bridge did break and they were both killed: and the second man's Faith was not disappointed and the first man's was.

(CL 3, 448)

On humility and humiliation

TO MARY WILLIS SHELBURNE MARCH 31, 1954

We should mind humiliation less if [we] were humbler.

(CL 3, 448)

The three patiences

TO MARY WILLIS SHELBURNE MARCH 31, 1954

How right you are to see that anger (even when directed against oneself) "worketh not the righteousness of God."* One must never be *either* content with, *or* impatient with, oneself. My old confessor** (now dead) used to impress on me the need for the 3 Patiences: patience with God, with my neighbor, with oneself.

*James 1:20

**Father Walter Adams

(CL 3, 449)

Note to a discouraged Christian apologist

TO CORBIN SCOTT CARNELL   JUNE 25, 1954

If you are losing your faith in argument, why trust the arguments that lead you to do so? (This skepticism about reason undercuts itself). Some people can be converted on rational grounds, but more can't. All rests with God, and one must not get flustered. If in a particular case He doesn't use *you* or *me* as His instrument, no doubt he has excellent reasons. No general conclusion follows.

(CL 3, 494)

LETTERS ON LIVING THE FAITH

Is sex the chief stumbling block of men?

TO MRS. "JONES"   SEPTEMBER 27, 1954

"Why has sex become man's chief stumbling block?" But has it? Or is it only the most *recognizable* of the stumbling blocks? I mean, we can mistake Pride for a good conscience, and Cruelty for zeal, but Idleness for the peace of God etc. But when Lust is upon us, then, owing to the obvious physical symptoms, we can't pretend it is anything else. Is it perhaps only the least *disguisable* of our dangers. At the same time I think there is something in what you say. If marriage is an image of the mystical marriage between Christ & the Church, then adultery is an image of apostasy. Also, all the sexual vices have this unfair advantage that the very temptation is itself pleasurable: whereas the temptations, say, to Anger or Cowardice are in themselves *un*pleasant.

(CL 3, 510)

To a correspondent whose spouse was not a Christian

TO MRS. JOHNSON   MARCH 2, 1955

It is right and inevitable that we should be much concerned about the salvation of those we love. But we must be careful not to expect or demand that their salvation should conform to some ready-made pattern of our own. Some Protestant sects have gone very wrong about this. They have a whole program of "conviction," "conversion" etc. marked out, the same for everyone, and will not believe that anyone can be saved who doesn't go through it "just so." But (see the last chapter of my *Problem of Pain*) God has His own way with each soul.

There is no evidence that St. John underwent the same kind of "conversion" as St. Paul. It's not essential to believe in the Devil: and I'm sure a man can get to Heaven without being accurate about Methuselah's age. Also, as Macdonald says "the time for *saying* comes seldom, the time for *being* is always here." What we practice, not (save at rare intervals) what we preach is usually our great contribution to the conversion of others.

(CL 3, 576)

Objections to religious teetotalism

TO MRS. JOHNSON   MARCH 16, 1955

I am afraid I am not going to be much help about all the religious bodies mentioned in your letter. . . . I have always in my books been concerned simply to put forward "mere" Christianity, and am no guide on these (most regrettable) "interdenominational" questions. I do however strongly object to the tyrannic and unscriptural insolence of anything that calls itself a Church and makes tee-totalism a condition of membership. Apart from the more serious objection (that Our Lord Himself turned water into wine and made wine the medium of the only rite He imposed on all His followers) it is so provincial (what I believe you people call "small town"). Don't they realize that Christianity arose in the Mediterranean world where, then as now, wine was as much part of the normal diet as bread?

(CL 3, 580)

On *"having to depend solely on God"*

TO MARY WILLIS SHELBURNE   DECEMBER 6, 1955

I feel it almost impossible to say anything (in my comfort and security—apparent security, for real security is in Heaven and thus earth affords only imitations) which would not sound horribly false and facile. Also, you know it all better than I do. I should in your place be (I *have* in similar places *been*) far more panic-stricken and even perhaps rebellious. For it is a dreadful truth that the state of (as you say) "having to depend solely on God" is what we all dread most. And of course that just shows how very much, how almost exclusively, we have been depending on things. But trouble goes so far back in our lives and is now so deeply ingrained, we *will* not turn to Him as long as He leaves us anything else to turn to. I suppose all one can say is that it was bound to come. In the hour of death and the day of judgment, what else shall we have? Perhaps when those moments come, they will feel happiest who have been forced (however unwittingly) to begin practicing it here on earth. It is good of Him to force us; but dear me, how hard to *feel* that it is good at the time.

(CL 3, 679)

The vast commercial drive called "Xmas"

TO FATHER PETER MILWARD   DECEMBER 17, 1955

Christmas cards in general and the whole vast commercial drive called "Xmas" are one of my pet abominations: I wish they could die away and leave the Christian feast unentangled. Not of course that even secular festivities are, on their own level, an evil: but the labored and organized jollity of this—the spurious childlikeness—the half-hearted and sometimes rather profane attempts to keep up some superficial connection with the Nativity—are disgusting.

(CL 3, 686)

In praise of Russian Orthodox services

TO MRS. JOHNSON   MARCH 13, 1956

Let's go on disagreeing but don't let us *judge*. What doesn't suit us may suit possible converts of a different type.

My model here is the behavior of the congregation at a "Russian Orthodox" service, where some sit, some lie on their faces, some stand, some kneel, some walk about, and *no one takes the slightest notice of what anyone else is doing.* That is good sense, good manners, and good Christianity. "Mind one's own business" is a good rule in religion as in other things.

(CL 3, 720)

On religious music

TO MRS. HALVORSON   MARCH 1956

Concerning hymn singing and organ playing: if they have been helpful and edified anyone, then the fact that they set my teeth on edge is infinitely unimportant.

One must first distinguish the effect which music has on people like me who are musically illiterate and get only the emotional effect, and that which it has on real musical scholars who perceive the structure and get an intellectual satisfaction as well.

Either of these effects is, I think, ambivalent from the religious point of view: i.e. *each* can be a preparation for or even a medium for meeting God but can also be a distraction and impediment. In that respect music is not different from a good many other things, human relations, landscape, poetry, philosophy. The most relevant one is wine which can be used sacramentally or for getting drunk or neutrally.

I think every *natural* thing which is not in itself sinful can become the servant of the spiritual life, but none is automatically so. When it is not, it becomes either just trivial (as music is to millions of people) or a dangerous idol. The emotional effect of music may be not only a distraction (to some people at some times) but a delusion: i.e. feeling certain emotions in church they mistake them for religious emotions when they may be wholly natural. That means that even genuinely religious emotion is only a servant. No soul is saved by having it or damned by lacking it. The love we are commended to have for God and our neighbor is a state of the *will*, not of the affections (though if they ever also play their part so much the better). So that the test of music or religion or even visions if one has them is always the same—do they make one more obedient, more God-centered, and neighbor-centered and *less self-centered*? "Though I speak with the tongues of Bach and Palestrina and have not charity etc!"*

*See Corinthians 13:1.

(CL 3, 731–732)

Intellectual assent vs. real belief

TO MARY VAN DEUSEN   MAY 14, 1956

Almost exactly the same thing that happened to you about the Incarnation happened to me a few years ago about the Forgiveness of Sins. Like you, I had *assented* to the doctrine years earlier and would have said I believed it. Then, one blessed day, it suddenly became real to me and made what I had previously called "belief" look absolutely unreal. It is a wonderful thing. But not, on inferior matters, so very uncommon. We all in one sense "believe" we are mortal: but until one's forties does one not *really* believe one is going to die? On the edge of a cliff can't one believe, and yet not really believe, that there's no danger? But certainly this real belief in the truths of our religion is a great gift from God. When in Hebrews "faith" is defined as "the substance of things hoped for," I would translate "substance" as "substantialness" or "solidity" or (almost) "palpableness."

(CL 3, 751)

The problem with erotic fantasies

TO KEITH MASSON   JUNE 3, 1956

For me the real evil of masturbation would be that it takes an appetite which, in lawful use, leads the individual out of himself to complete (and correct) his own personality in that of another (and finally in children and even grandchildren) and turns it back: sends the man back into the prison of himself, there to keep a harem of imaginary brides. And this harem, once admitted, works against his *ever* getting out and really uniting with a real woman. For the harem is always accessible, always subservient, calls for no sacrifices or adjustments, and can be endowed with erotic and psychological attractions which no real woman can rival. Among those shadowy brides he is always adored, always the perfect lover: no demand is made on his unselfishness, no mortification ever imposed on his vanity. In the end, they become merely the medium through which he increasingly adores himself....

The true exercise of imagination, in my view, is (a) To help us to understand other people (b) To respond to, and, some of us, to produce, art. But it has also a bad use: to provide for us, in shadowy form, a substitute for virtues, successes, distinctions etc. which ought to be sought *outside* in the real world—e.g. picturing all I'd do if I were rich instead of earning and saving. Masturbation involves this abuse of imagination in erotic matters (which I think bad in itself) and thereby encourages a similar abuse of it in all spheres. After all, almost the *main* work of life is to *come out* of ourselves, out of the little, dark prison we are all born in. Masturbation is to be avoided as *all* things to be avoided which retard this process. The danger is that of coming to *love* the prison.

(CL 3, 758–759)

On living with adversity

TO MARY WILLIS SHELBURNE   JUNE 14, 1956

The great thing with unhappy times is to take them bit by bit, hour by hour, like an illness. It is seldom the *present*, the exact present, that is unbearable.

(CL 3, 761–762)

On human suffering and Christ's suffering

TO MARY MARGARET MCCASLIN   NOVEMBER 15, 1956

I will indeed pray for you: I did so already, and will do so more. You have made a great sacrifice for conscience's sake. Such things, we may be sure, enrich one: but God knows it doesn't *feel* like it at the time. It did not, even for our Lord himself, in Gethsemane. I always try to remember what MacDonald said "The Son of God died not that we might not suffer but that our sufferings might become like His."

But of course the real difficulty is not in rising to this point of view but in *staying* there. One does it—and ten minutes later it all has to be done over again. And one gets so *tired*, doesn't one? . . . May God strengthen you, as only He can.

(CL 3, 806)

"God gives where He finds empty hands."

TO MARY WILLIS SHELBURNE   MARCH 31, 1958

St. Augustine says "God gives where He finds empty hands." A man whose hands are full of parcels can't receive a gift. Perhaps these parcels are not always sins or earthly cares, but sometimes our own fussy attempts to worship Him in *our* way. Incidentally, what most often interrupts my own prayers is not great distractions but tiny ones—things one will have to do or avoid in the course of the next hour.

(CL 3, 930–931)

To a correspondent who asked for a book on egocentrism

TO EDWARD LOFSTROM   MARCH 8, 1959

One can argue against egoism, but then egoism is not his trouble. If he were a real egoist he would be either blissfully unconscious of the fact or else fully convinced that egoism was the rational attitude. You, on the other hand, suffer from a more than ordinary horror of egoism which you share with us all. And therefore, as you will see, the thing you need is not to think more or better about it but to think less: to *act* unselfishly—that is, charitably and justly—and leave the state of your feelings for God to deal with in His own way and His own time. And this of course you know better than I do.

But how to do it? For the very effort to forget something is itself a remembering of that something! I think, if I were in your shoes I should try to regard this sense of self-imprisonment not at all as a sin but as a mere tribulation, like rheumatism, to be endured in the same way. It has no doubt its medical side: diet, exercise, and recreations might all be considered. And, though this is a hard saying, your early upbringing may have something to do with it. Great piety in the parents *can* produce in the child a mistaken sense of guilt: may lead him to regard as sin what is really not sin at all but merely the fact that he is a boy and not a mature Christian. At any rate, remember "I cannot turn one hair black or white: but I can brush my hair daily and go to the barber at regular intervals." In other words we must divert our efforts from our general condition or frame of mind (which we can't alter by direct action of the will) to what is in our power—our words and acts. Try to remember that the "bottomless sea" can't hurt us as long as we keep on *swimming*. You will be in my prayers.

(CL 3, 1027–1028)

On giving alms

TO MARY WILLIS SHELBURNE   OCTOBER 26, 1962

I do most thoroughly agree with your father's principle about alms. It will not bother me in the hour of death to reflect that I have been "had for a sucker" by any number of impostors; but it would be a torment to know that one had refused even *one* person in need. After all, the parable of the sheep and goats* makes our duty perfectly plain, doesn't it. Another thing that annoys me is when people say "Why did you give that man money? He'll probably go and drink it." My reply is "But if I'd kept [it] *I* should probably have drunk it."

*Matthew 25:31–46

(CL 3, 1376)

On resisting change

TO MARY VAN DEUSEN   NOVEMBER 21, 1962

I think I share, to excess, your feeling about a move. By nature I demand from the arrangements of this world just that permanence which God has expressly refused to give them. It is not merely the nuisance and expense of any big change in one's way of life that I dread. It is also the psychological uprooting and the feeling—to me, and to you, intensely unwelcome—of having ended a chapter. One more portion of oneself slipping away into the past! I would like everything to be immemorial—to have the same old horizons, the same gender, the same smells and sound, always there changeless. The old wine is to me always better. That is, I desire the "abiding city" where I will know it is not and ought not to be found. I suppose all these changes should prepare us for the far greater change which has drawn nearer even since I began this letter. We must "sit light" not only to life itself but to all its phases. The useless word is "Encore!"

(CL 3, 1383)

On forgiveness as a process

TO PHOEBE HESKETH   JUNE 14, 1960

The real trouble about the duty of forgiveness is that you do it with all your might on Monday and then find on Wednesday that it hasn't stayed put and all has to be done over again.

(CL 3, 1162)

On dealing with family members

TO MARY WILLIS SHELBURNE   FEBRUARY 24, 1961

I hope and pray you will be able to do them some good, but probably if you do, it will not be by any voluntary and conscious actions. Your prayers for them will be more use. Probably the safe rule will be "When in doubt what to do or say, do or say nothing." I feel this *very* much with my stepsons.* I so easily *meddle* and *gas*: when all the time what will really influence them, for good or ill, is not anything I do or say but what I *am*. And this unfortunately one can't know and can't much alter, though God can. Two rules from William Law** must be always before our minds.

1. "There can be no surer proof of a confirmed pride than a belief that one is sufficiently humble."
2. "I earnestly beseech all who conceive they have suffered an affront to believe that it is very much less than they suppose."

*David and Douglas Gresham, sons of Joy Davidman Gresham Lewis, who was married to Lewis from 1956 until her death in 1960

**William Law, *A Serious Call to a Devout and Holy Life*

(CL 3, 1242–1243)

Avoid fixating on the past

TO MARY WILLIS SHELBURNE   JUNE 5, 1961

We must beware of the Past, mustn't we? I mean that any fixing of the mind on old evils beyond what is absolutely necessary for repenting our own sins and forgiving those of others is certainly useless and usually bad for us. Notice in Dante that the lost souls are entirely concerned with their past. Not so the saved. This is one of the dangers of being, like you and me, old. There's so much past, now, isn't there? And so little else. But we must try very hard not to keep on endlessly chewing the cud. We must look forward more eagerly to sloughing that old skin off forever—metaphors getting a bit mixed here, but you know what I mean.

(CL 3, 1274)

On temptations to sin and confessions of sin

TO HARVEY KARLSEN   OCTOBER 13, 1961

Of course I have had and still have plenty of temptations. Frequent and regular prayer, and frequent and regular Communions, are a great help, whether they *feel* at the time as if they were doing you good or whether they don't.

I also found great help in monthly confession to a wise old clergyman.*

Perhaps, however, the most important thing is to *keep on*: not to be discouraged however often one yields to the temptation, but always to pick yourself up again and ask forgiveness. In reviewing your sins don't either exaggerate them or minimize them. Call them by their ordinary names and try to see them as you would see the same faults in somebody else—no special blackening or whitewashing. Remember the condition on which we are promised forgiveness: we shall always be forgiven provided that we forgive all who sin against us. If we do that we have nothing to fear: if we don't, all else will be in vain. Of course there are other helps which are mere commonsense. We must learn by experience to avoid either trains of thought or social situations which *for us* (not necessarily for everyone) lead to temptations. Like motoring—don't wait till the last moment before you put on the brakes but put them on, gently and quietly, while the danger is still a good way off.

*Father Walter Adams

(CL 3, 1285–1286)

Questions About Christian Theology and Morality

C. S. LEWIS

How can an all-good God produce a world with evil?

TO ARTHUR GREEVESSEPTEMBER 12, 1933

I have been thinking all morning over your question about God and evil which is very far from being "elementary" to me—or for that matter, I suppose, to the angels. If I understand you rightly you are not *primarily* concerned with the sort of logical problem as how the All-Good can produce evil, or produce a world in which there is evil, but with a more personal, practical, and intimate problem as to how far God can sympathize with our evil will as well as with our good—or, to draw it milder, *whether* he does.

I should begin, I think, by objecting to an expression you use: "God must have a potentiality of His opposite—evil." For this I would substitute the idea which someone had in the Middle Ages who defined God as "*That which has no opposite*" i.e. we live in a world of clashes, good and evil, true and false, pleasant and painful, body and spirit, time and eternity etc., but God is not simply (so to speak) *one* of the two clashes but the ultimate thing beyond them all—just as in our constitution the King is neither the Prime Minister nor the Leader of the Opposition, but the thing behind them which alone enables these to be a lawful government and an opposition—or just as space is neither bigness or smallness but that in which the distinctions of big and small arise. This then is my first point. That Evil is not something outside and "*over against*" God, but *in some way* included under Him.

My second point seems to be in direct contradiction to this first one, and is (in scriptural language) as follows: that God "is the Father of Lights and in Him is *no darkness at all*."* *In some way* there is no evil whatever in God. He is pure Light. All the *heat* that in us is lust or anger in Him is cool light—eternal morning, eternal freshness, eternal springtime: never disturbed, never strained. Go out on any perfect morning in early summer before the world is awake and see, not the thing itself, but the material symbol of it.

Well, these are our two starting points. *In one way* . . . God includes evil, in another way he does not. What are we to do next? My beginning of the "next" will be to deny another remark of yours—where you say "no good without evil." This on my view is absolutely untrue: but the opposite "no evil without good" is absolutely true. I will try to explain what I mean by an analogy.

Supposing you are taking a dog on a lead [leash] through a turnstile or past a post. You know what happens (apart from his usual ceremonies in passing a post!). He tries to go to the wrong side and gets his lead looped round the post. *You* see that he can't do it, and therefore pull him back. You pull him *back* because you want to enable him to go *forward*. He wants exactly the same thing—namely to go *forward*: for that very reason he resists your pull *back*, or, if he is an obedient dog, yields to it reluctantly as a matter of duty which seems to him to be quite in opposition to his own will: though *in fact* it is only by yielding to you that he will ever succeed in getting where he wants.

Now if the dog were a theologian he would regard his own will as a *sin* to which he was tempted, and therefore an *evil*: and he might go on to ask whether you understand and "contained" his evil. If he did you could only reply "My dear dog, if by your will you mean what you really want to do, viz. to get forward along the road, I not only understand this desire but *share* it. Forward is exactly where I want you to go. If by your will, on the other hand, you mean your will to pull against the collar and try to force yourself forward in a direction which is no use—why I *understand* it of course: but just because I understand it (and the whole situation, which you *don't* understand) I cannot possibly share it. In fact the more I sympathize with your *real* wish—that is, the wish to get on—the less can I sympathize (in the sense of "share" or "agree with") your resistance to the collar: for I see that this is actually rendering the attainment of your real wish impossible."

I don't know if you will agree at once that this is a parallel to the situation between God and man: but I will work it out on the assumption that you do. Let us go back to the original question—whether and, if so, in what sense God contains, say, my evil will—or "understands" it. The answer is God not only understands but *shares* the desire which is at the root of all my evil: the desire for complete and ecstatic happiness. He made me for no other purpose than to enjoy it. But He knows, and I do not, how it can be really and permanently attained. He knows that most of *my* personal attempts to reach it are actually putting it further and further out of my reach. With these therefore He cannot sympathize or "agree": His sympathy with my *real* will makes that impossible. (He may *pity* my misdirected struggles, but that is another matter.) The practical results seem to be two.

1. I may always feel looking back on any past sin that in the very heart of my evil passion there was something that God approves and wants me to feel not less but more. Take a sin of Lust. The overwhelming thirst for *rapture* was good and even divine: it has not got to be unsaid (so to speak) and recanted. But it will never be quenched as I tried to quench it. If I refrain—if I submit to the collar and come round the right side of the lamppost—God will be guiding me as quickly as He can to where I shall get what I really wanted all the time. It will not be very like what I now think I want: but it will be more like it than some suppose. In any case it will be the real thing,

not a consolation prize or substitute. If I had it I should not need to fight against sensuality as something impure: rather I should spontaneously turn away from it as something dull, cold, abstract, and artificial. This, I think, is how the doctrine applies to past sins.

2. On the other hand, when we are thinking of a sin in the future, i.e. when we are tempted, we must remember that *just because* God wants for us what we really want and knows the only way to get it, therefore He must, in a sense, be quite ruthless towards sin. He is not like a human authority who can be begged off or caught in an indulgent mood. The more He loves you the more determined He must be to pull you back from your way which leads nowhere into His way which leads where you want to go. Hence MacDonald's words "The *all-punishing, all-pardoning* Father." You may go the wrong way again, and again He may forgive you: as the dog's master may extricate the dog after he has tied the whole lead round the lamppost. But there is no hope in the end of getting where you want to go except by going God's way . . .

Only because he has laid up *real* goods for us to desire are we able to go wrong by snatching at them in greedy, misdirected ways. The truth is that evil is not a real *thing* at all, like God. It is simply good *spoiled*. That is why I say there can be good without evil, but no evil without good. You know what the biologists mean by a parasite—an animal that lives on another animal. Evil is a *parasite*. It is there only because good is there for it to spoil and confuse.

Thus you may well feel that God understands our temptations—understands them a great deal more than we do. But don't forget MacDonald again—"*Only God understands evil and hates it.*" Only the dog's master knows how useless it is to try to get on with the lead knotted round the lamppost. This is why we must be prepared to find God implacably and immovably forbidding what may seem to us very small and trivial things. But He knows whether they are really small and trivial. How small some of the things that doctors forbid would seem to an ignoramus.

*I John 1:5

(CL 2, 121–125)

On the origins of evil: "The black fire of self-imprisonment"

TO JOYCE PEARCE   JULY 20, 1943

Go to the top of the class! You seem to have evolved the answer of the best theologians on your own: and I agree with it.

You will find what I have to say about it in my little book *The Problem of Pain*. It is to me inconceivable that Nature as we see it is either what God intended *or* merely evil: it looks like a good thing spoiled.

The doctrine of the Fall (both of man and of some "gods," "eldils,"* or "angels") is the only satisfactory explanation. Evil begins, in a universe where all was good, from free will, which was permitted because it makes possible the greatest good of all. The corruption of the first sinner consists not in choosing some evil thing (there are no evil things for him to choose) but in preferring a lesser good (himself) before a great (God). The Fall is, in fact, Pride. The possibility of this wrong preference is inherent in the very fact of having, or being, a self at all. But though freedom is real it is not infinite. Every choice reduces a little one's freedom to choose the next time. There therefore comes a time when the creature is fully *built*, irrevocably attached either to God or to itself. This irrevocableness is what we call Heaven or Hell. Every conscious agent is finally committed in the long run: i.e. it rises above freedom into willed, but henceforth unalterable, union with God, or else sinks below freedom into the black fire of self-imprisonment.

*Angel-like creatures in Lewis's Ransom trilogy

(CL 2, 584–585)

Seeing the natural through the lens of the supernatural

TO DOM BEDE GRIFFITHS   MAY 10, 1945

I too have been very much occupied by the idea of the New Creation. I'm absolutely with you. New heavens and earth—the resurrection of the body—how we have neglected these doctrines and indeed left the romantics and even the Marxists to step into the gap.

I'm working at a book on Miracles at present in which this theme will play a large part. And here's a funny thing. To write a book on miracles, which are in a sense invasions of Nature, has made me realize Nature herself as I've never done before. You don't *see* Nature till you believe in the Supernatural: don't get the full, hot, salty tang of her except by contrast with the pure water from beyond the world. Those who mistake Nature for the All are just those who can never realize her as a *particular creature* with her own flawed, terrible, beautiful individuality. No time to develop this now—but I thought you'd like to know the thoughts I am drunk with.

(CL 2, 648)

On the need to stamp out "religion"

TO SISTER PENELOPE   MAY 28, 1945

The truth is we shall never get on till we have stamped out "religion." "Religion" as it is called—the vague slush of humanitarian idealism, Emersonian Pantheism, democratic politics and material progressiveness with a few Christian names and formulae added to taste like pepper and salt—is almost the great enemy. If one can't talk to a Christian then give me a real believing member of some other religion or an honest clearheaded skeptic like J.[ohn] S.[tuart] Mill. One can at least get sense out of them.

(CSL 2, 657)

Calvinism

TO MR. N. FRIDAMA   FEBRUARY 15, 1946

On Calvinism. Both the statement that our final destination is already settled and the view that it still may be either Heaven or Hell, seem to me to imply the ultimate reality of Time, which I don't believe in. The controversy is one I can't join on either side for I think that in the real (Timeless) world it is meaningless.

(CL 2, 703)

Hell as a state of mind

TO ARTHUR GREEVES   MAY 13, 1946

About Hell. All I have ever said is that the N[ew] T[estament] plainly implies the possibility of some being finally left in "the outer darkness."* Whether this means (horror of horror) being left to a purely mental existence, left with nothing at all but one's own envy, prurience, resentment, loneliness and self-conceit, or whether there is still some sort of environment, something you could call a world or a reality, I would never pretend to know. But I wouldn't put the question in the form "do I believe in an *actual* Hell." One's own mind is actual enough. If it doesn't seem fully actual *now* that is because you can always escape from it a bit into the physical world—look out of the window, smoke a cigarette, go to sleep. But when there is nothing for you *but* your own mind (no body to go to sleep, no books or landscape, no sounds, no drugs) it will be as actual as—as—well, as a coffin is actual to a man buried alive.

*Matthew 8:12; 22:13; 25:30

(CL 2, 710)

On Jesus Christ as All-God and All-Man

TO MRS. FRANK L. JONES   FEBRUARY 23, 1947

1. The doctrine that Our Lord was God and man does not mean that He was a human body which had God instead of the normal human soul. It means that a real man (human body and human soul) was in Him so united with the 2nd Person of the Trinity as to make one Person: just as in you and me a complete anthropoid animal (animal body and animal "soul" i.e. instincts, sensations, etc.) is so united with an immortal rational soul as to be one person. In other words, if the Divine Son had been removed from Jesus what would have been left would have been not a corpse but a living man.

2. This human soul in Him was unswervingly united to the God in Him in that which makes a personality one, namely Will. But it had the feelings of any normal man: hence could be tempted, could fear, etc. Because of these feelings it could pray "if it be possible, let this cup pass from me": because of its perfect union with His Divine Nature it unswervingly answered "Nevertheless, not as I will but as thou wilt." The Matthew passage and the John passage both make clear this unity of will. The Matthew one gives in addition the human feelings.

3. God could, had He pleased, have been incarnate in a man of iron nerves, the Stoic sort who lets no sigh escape Him.

Of His great humility He chose to be incarnate in a man of delicate sensibilities who wept at the grave of Lazarus and sweated blood in Gethsemane. Otherwise we should have missed the great lesson that it is by his will alone that a man is good or bad, and that feelings are not, in themselves, of any importance. We should also have missed the all important help of knowing that He has faced all that the weakest of us face, has shared not only the strength of our nature but every weakness of it except sin. If He had been incarnate in a man of immense natural courage, that would have been for many of us almost the same as His not being incarnate at all.

(CL 2, 764–765)

Sin-as-it-is vs. one's experience of sin

TO EDWARD T. DELL   MARCH 28, 1949

By *experience* I mean "That part or result of any event which is presented to consciousness." Thus in a Toothache the total event is a complex physiological, bio-chemical, and (in the long run) atomic event: what is presented to consciousness, i.e. the *Pain*, I call an *experience*.

Thus to your question (1.) I reply *Sin* is the turning away of the will from God. But the *experience* of sin will differ in different people: e.g. to an uninstructed person it may appear in consciousness merely as disobeying human authority, or taking a legitimate indulgence. That sin-as-it-really-is is *ever* fully present to human (as opposed to diabolical) consciousness at the moment of commission, I doubt. The rebellion of the will is nearly always accompanied with *some* fogging of the intelligence....

I hope some day to write an autobiography* which will tell *what I know* (= the experience) of my own conversion. But the real event, as known to God, will differ from this as much as the total event "decaying tooth" differs from the pain.

Surprised by Joy was published in 1955.

(CL 2, 928–929)

Time is a defect of reality

TO EDWARD T. DELL   FEBRUARY 4, 1949

I firmly believe that God's life is non temporal. Time is a defect of reality since by its very nature any temporal being loses each moment of its life to get the next—the moments run through us as if we were sieves! God forbid that we should think God to be like that. On the eternal Now read Boethius, von Hügel's *Eternal Life* etc. Also St. Peter who adds to the old maxim "1000 years in His sight are but as a day" the very important opposite "and a day as 1000 years."

(CL 2, 915)

Why does a good God allow evil into the world?

TO ARTHUR GREEVES   JULY 6, 1949

I do not hold that God "sends" sickness or war in the sense in which He sends us all good things. Hence in Luke 13:16 Our Lord clearly attributes a disease not to the action of His Father but to that of Satan. I think you are quite right. All suffering arises from sin.

The sense in which it is also God's will seems to me twofold (a) The one you mention: that God willed the free will of men and angels in spite of His knowledge that it could lead in some cases to sin and thence to suffering: i.e. He thought Freedom worth creating even at that price. It is like when a mother allows a small child to walk on its own instead of holding it by her hand. She knows it may fall, but learning to walk on one's own is worth a few falls. When it does fall this is in one sense contrary to the mother's will: but the general situation in which falls are possible *is* the mother's will. (In fact, as you and I have so often said before "in one way it is, in another way it isn't!")

(b) The world is so made that the sins of one inflict suffering on another. Now I don't think God allows this to happen at random. I think that if He knew that the suffering entailed on innocent A by the sins of B would be (in the deep sense & the long run) *bad* for A, He would shield A from it. And in that sense I think it is sometimes God's will that A should go through this suffering. The supreme case is the suffering that our sins entailed on Christ. When Christ saw that suffering drawing near He prayed (Luke 22:42) "If thou be willing, remove this cup from me: nevertheless not my will but thine." This seems to me to make it quite clear that the crucifixion was (in the very qualified sense which I've tried to define) God's will.

(CL 2, 956–957)

Two letters to Edward T. Dell

(Dell wrote to ask if we call something evil because we apply the wrong criteria, such as calling an untimely death evil on the assumption that it would be better to live forever.)

IS EVIL AN ILLUSION?

December 19, 1949

I don't think the idea that evil is an illusion helps. Because surely it is a (real) evil that the illusion of evil should exist. When I am pursued in a nightmare by a crocodile the pursuit and the crocodile are illusions: but it is a real nightmare, and that seems a real evil. (Whenever one says "This isn't a real so-and-so," is it not a real something else? e.g. if this is not a real pink rat it is real delirium, if this pupil is not a real sufferer from headache he is a real liar—and so on).

(CL 2, 1010)

January 30, 1950

I think we mean very nearly the same. Evil is certainly not a "Thing." But many states of affairs, or relations between things, are regrettable, ought not to have occurred, and ought to be removed. And "Evil" is an elliptical symbol for this fact.

(CL 3, 8)

On physical healing by spiritual means

TO MARY VAN DEUSEN   DECEMBER 7, 1950

I am not clear *what* question you are asking me about spiritual healing. That this gift was promised to the Church is certain from Scripture. Whether any instance of it is a real instance, or chance, or even (as might happen in this wicked world) fraud, is a question only to be decided by the evidence in that particular case. And unless one is a doctor one is not likely to be able to judge the evidence. Very often, I expect, one is not called upon to do so. Anything like a sudden *furore* about it in one district, especially if accompanied by a publicity campaign on modern commercial lines, would be to me suspect: but even then I might be wrong. On the whole, my attitude would be that any claim *may* be true, and that it is not my duty to decide whether it is.

(CL 3, 69)

To a critic of the Christian doctrine of Atonement

TO WENDELL W. WATTERS   OCTOBER 25, 1951

I am not surprised that a man who agreed with me in *Screwtape* (ethics served with an imaginative seasoning) might disagree with me when I wrote about religion. We can hardly discuss the whole matter by post, can we?

I'll only make one shot. When people object, as you do, that if Jesus was God as well as Man, then He had an unfair advantage which deprives Him for them of all value, it seems to me as if a man struggling in the water should refuse a rope thrown to him by another who had one foot on the bank, saying "Oh but you have an unfair advantage"; it is because of that advantage that He can help.

But all good wishes: we must just differ: in charity I hope. You must not be *angry* with me for believing you know: I'm not angry with you!

(CL 3, 143)

Pain as punishment vs. pain as palliative

TO MARY VAN DEUSEN   JANUARY 31, 1952

That suffering is not *always* sent as a punishment is clearly established for believers by the book of Job and by John 9:1–4. That it *sometimes* is, is suggested by parts of the Old Testament and Revelation. It would certainly be most dangerous to assume that any given pain was penal. I believe that all pain is contrary to God's will, absolutely but not relatively. When I am taking a thorn out of my finger (or a child's finger) the pain is "absolutely" contrary to my will: i.e. if I could have chosen a situation without pain I would have done so. But I *do* will what caused pain, relatively to the given situation: i.e. granted the thorn I prefer the pain to leaving the thorn where it is. A mother smacking a child would be in the same position: she would rather cause it this pain than let it go on pulling the cat's tail, but she would like it better if no situation which demands a smack had arisen.

(CL 3, 163)

Can unbelievers find salvation?

TO MARY VAN DEUSEN   JANUARY 31, 1952

On the heathen, see I Tim. 4:10. Also in Matt. 25:31–46 the people don't sound as if they were believers. Also the doctrine of Christ's descending into Hell* and preaching to the dead: that would be outside time, and include those who died long after Him as well as those who died before He was born as Man. I don't think we know the details: we must just stick to the view that (a.) All justice and mercy will be done, (b.) But that nevertheless it is our duty to do all we can to convert unbelievers.

[Lewis's note] i.e. Hades, the land of the dead: not Gehenna, the land of the lost

(CL 3, 163)

High Church, Low Church, and "Deep Church"

TO THE EDITOR OF THE *CHURCH TIMES*

To a layman, it seems obvious that what unites the Evangelical and the Anglo-Catholic against the "Liberal" or "Modernist" is something very clear and momentous, namely, the fact that both are thoroughgoing supernaturalists, who believe in the Creation, the Fall, the Incarnation, the Resurrection, the Second Coming, and the Four Last Things. This unites them not only with one another, but with the Christian religion as understood *ubique et ab omnibus*.*

The point of view from which this agreement seems less important than their divisions, or than the gulf which separates both from any non-miraculous version of Christianity, is to me unintelligible. Perhaps the trouble is that as supernaturalists, whether "Low" or "High" Church, thus taken together, they lack a name. May I suggest "Deep Church"; or, if that fails in humility, Baxter's "mere Christians"?**

*Reference to the Latin phrase which means "believed everywhere, by all, at all times"

**Richard Baxter, a seventeenth-century English Puritan church leader

(CL 3, 164)

The *"indiscussable" question of free will and predestination*

TO MARY VAN DEUSEN   OCTOBER 20, 1952

All that Calvinist question—Free will and Predestination, is to my mind indiscussable, insoluble. Of course (say us) if a man repents God will accept him. Ah yes (say they), but the fact of his repenting shows that God has already moved him to do so. This at any rate leaves us with the fact that in *any concrete case* the question never arises as a practical one. But I suspect it is really a *meaningless* question. The difference between Freedom and Necessity is fairly clear on the bodily level: we know the difference between making our teeth chatter and just finding them chattering with the cold. It begins to be less clear when we talk about human love (leaving out the erotic kind). "Do I like him because I choose or because I must?"—there are cases where this has an answer, but others where it seems to me to mean nothing. When we carry it up to relations between God and Man, has the distinction become perhaps nonsensical? After all, when we are most free, it is only with a freedom God has given us: and when our will is most influenced by Grace, it is still *our will*. And if what *our will* does is not voluntary, and if "voluntary" does not mean "free," what are we talking about? I'd leave it alone. Blessings.

(CL 3, 237)

Providence vs. coincidence

TO VERA GERBERT   MARCH 23, 1953

Now as to your other story, about Isaiah 66? It doesn't really matter whether the Bible was open at that page thru' a miracle or through some (unobserved) natural cause. We think it matters because we tend to call the second alternative "chance." But when you come to think of [it] there can be no such thing as chance from God's point of view. Since He is omniscient His acts have no consequences which He has not foreseen and taken into account and intended. Suppose it was the draft from the window that blew your Bible open at Isaiah 66. Well, that current of air was linked up with the whole history of weather from the beginning of the world and you may be quite sure that the result it had for you at that moment (like all its other results) was intended and allowed for in the act of creation. "Not one sparrow,"* you know the rest. So *of course* the message was addressed to you. To suggest that your eye fell on it *without* this intention, is to suggest that you could take

Him by surprise. Fiddle-de-dee! This is not Predestination: your will is perfectly free: but all physical events are adapted to fit in as God sees best with the free actions He knows we are going to do. There's something about this in *Screwtape*.

Meanwhile, *courage*! Your moments of nervousness are not your real self, only medical phenomena. All blessings.

*Matthew 10:29

(CL 3, 311–312)

Sin is a matter of bad choices, not bad reasoning

TO ELSIE SNICKERS   MAY 18, 1953

No. I don't think sin is completely accounted for by faulty reasoning nor that it can be completely cured by re-education. That view has, indeed, been put forward: by Socrates and, in the early 19th Century, by Godwin. But I think it overlooked the (to me) obviously central fact that our *will* is not necessarily determined by our *reason*. If it were, then, as you say, what are called "sins" would not be sins at all but only mistakes, and would require not repentances but merely correction.

But surely daily experience shows that it is just not so. A man's reason sees perfectly clearly that the resulting discomfort and inconvenience will far outweigh the pleasure of the ten minutes in bed. Yet he stays in bed: not at all because his reason is deceived but because desire is stronger than reason. A woman knows that the sharp "last word" in an argument will produce a serious quarrel which was the very thing she had intended to avoid when that argument began and which may permanently destroy her happiness. Yet she says it: not at all because her reason is deceived but because the desire to score a point is at the moment stronger than her reason. People—you and I among them—constantly choose between two courses of action the one which we know to be the worse: because, at the moment, we *prefer* the gratification of our anger, lust, sloth, greed, vanity, curiosity or cowardice, not only to the known will of God but even to what we know will make for our own real comfort and security. If you don't recognize this, then I must solemnly assure that either [you] are an angel, or else are still living in "a fool's paradise": a world of illusion.

Of course, it is true that many people are so mis-educated or so psychopathic that their freedom of action is very much curtailed and their responsibility therefore very small. We cannot remember that too much when we are tempted to judge harshly the acts of other people whose difficulties we don't know. But we know that some of *our own acts* have sprung from evil *will* (proud, resentful, cowardly, envious, lascivious or spiteful will) although we knew better, and that what we need is not—or not *only*—re-education but repentance, God's forgiveness, and His Grace to help us to do better next time. Until one has faced this fact one is a child.

And it is not the function of psychotherapy to make us face *this*. Its work is the non-moral aspects of conduct. You must not go to the psychologists for *spiritual* guidance. (One goes to the dentist to cure one's toothache, not to teach one in what spirit to bear it if it cannot be cured: for that you must go to God and God's spokesmen).

(CL 3, 329–330)

Does God choose us or do we choose God?

TO MRS. EMILY MCLAY   AUGUST 3, 1953

I take it as a first principle that we must not interpret any one part of Scripture so that it contradicts other parts, and specially we must not use an apostle's teaching to contradict that of Our Lord. Whatever St. Paul may have meant, we must not reject the parable of the sheep and the goats (Matt. 25:30–46). There, you see there is nothing about Predestination or even about Faith—all depends on works. But how this is to be reconciled with St. Paul's teaching, or with other sayings of Our Lord, I frankly confess I don't know. Even St. Peter you know admits that he was stumped by the Pauline epistles (II Peter 3:16–17).

What I *think* is this. Everyone looking back on *his own* conversion must feel—and I am sure the feeling is in some sense true—"It is not I who have done this. I did not choose Christ: He chose me. It is all free grace, which I have done nothing to earn." That is the Pauline account: and I am sure it is the only true account of every conversion *from the inside*. Very well. It then seems to us logical and natural to turn this personal experience into a general rule, "All conversions depend on God's choice."

But this I believe is exactly what we must not do: for generalizations are legitimate only when we are dealing with matters to which our faculties are adequate. Here, we are not. *How* our individual experiences are *in reality* consistent with (a) Our idea of Divine justice, (b) The parable I've just quoted and lots of other passages, we don't and can't know: what is clear is that *we* can't find a consistent formula. I think we must take a leaf out of the scientist's book. They are quite familiar with the fact that, for example, Light has to be regarded *both* as a wave in the ether and as a stream of particles. No one can make these two views consistent. Of course reality must be self-consistent: but till (if ever) we can *see* the consistency it is better to hold two inconsistent views than to ignore one side of the evidence.

The real inter-relation between God's omnipotence and Man's freedom is something we can't find out. Looking at the Sheep & the Goats every man can be quite sure that every kind act he does will be accepted by Christ. Yet, equally, we all do feel sure that all the good in us comes from Grace. We have to leave it at that. I find the best plan is to take the Calvinist view of my own virtues and other people's vices: and the other view of my own vices and other people's virtues. But tho' there is much to be *puzzled* about, there is nothing to be *worried* about. It is plain from Scripture that, in whatever sense the Pauline doctrine is true, it is not true in any sense which *excludes* its (apparent) opposite.

You know what [Martin] Luther said: "Do you doubt if you are chosen? Then say your prayers and you may conclude that you are."

(CL 3, 354–355)

God's absolute will vs. relative will

TO MARY VAN DEUSEN   NOVEMBER 28, 1953

As to whether God ever wills suffering, I think he [Van Deusen's rector] is confused. We must distinguish in God, and even in ourselves, absolute will from relative will. No one absolutely wills to have a tooth out, but many will to have a tooth out *rather than* to go on with a toothache. Surely in the same way God never absolutely wills the least suffering for any creature, but may will it *rather than* some alternative: e.g. He willed the crucifixion rather than that Man should go unredeemed (and so it was *not*, in all senses, His will that the cup should pass from His Son).

(CL 3, 379)

Can Satan create evil?

TO BELLE ALLEN   NOVEMBER 1, 1954

I think it would be dangerous to suppose that Satan had created all the creatures that are disagreeable or dangerous to us for (a) those creatures, if they could think, would have just the same reason for thinking that *we* were created by Satan. (b) I don't think evil, in the strict sense, can *create*. It can spoil something that Another has created. Satan may have corrupted other creatures as well as us. Part of the corruption in us might be the unreasoning horror and disgust we feel at some creatures quite apart from any harm they can do us. (I can't abide a spider myself.) We have scriptural authority for Satan's originating diseases—see Luke 13:16.

(CL 3, 520)

C. S. LEWIS

The suffering of the innocent and the suffering of the wicked

TO BELLE ALLEN　　　　　　NOVEMBER 1, 1954

Do you know, the suffering of the innocent is *less* of a problem to me very often than that of the wicked. It sounds absurd: but I've met so many innocent sufferers who seem to be gladly offering their pain to God in Christ as part of the Atonement, so patient, so meek, even so at peace, and so unselfish that we can hardly doubt they are being, as St. Paul says, "made perfect by suffering."* On the other hand I meet selfish egoists in whom suffering seems to produce only resentment, hate, blasphemy, and more egoism. They are the real problem.

*Hebrew 2:10

(CL 3, 520)

For Christians, nothing happens by chance

TO MRS. D. JESSUP　　　　　　MARCH 2, 1955

Oh what a rare blessing to have a Christian psychotherapist! I don't think your question whether these ones were brought into your life by "a whimsical fate" or by God, need detain you long. Once one believes in God at all, surely the question is meaningless? Suppose that in a novel a character gets killed in a railway accident. Is his death due to change (e.g. the signals being wrong) or to the novelist? Well of course, both. The chance is *the way* the novelist removes the character at the exact moment his story requires. There's a good line in Spenser to quote to oneself: "It chanced (almighty God that chance did guide)."

(CL 3, 574–575)

How much larger is reality than our outlines of faith?

TO DOM BEDE GRIFFITHS   FEBRUARY 8, 1956

One often wonders how different the content of our faith will look when we see it in the total context. Might it be as if one were living on an infinite earth? Further knowledge would leave our map of, say, the Atlantic quite *correct*, but if it turned out to be the estuary of a great river—and the continent through which that river flowed turned out to be itself an island—off the shores of a still greater continent—and so on! You see what I mean? Not one jot of Revelation will be proved false: but so many new truths might be added.

(CL 3, 703–704)

"Culture" too shall pass away

TO MARY VAN DEUSEN   APRIL 2, 1956

I'm a little, not unamusedly, surprised that my *S. by J.* [*Surprised by Joy*] causes you envy. I doubt if you would really have enjoyed my life much more than your own. And the whole modern world ludicrously over-values books and learning and what (I loathe the word) they call "culture." And of course "culture" itself is the greatest sufferer by this error: for second things are always corrupted when they are put first. Never forget this: souls are immortal, and your children and grandchildren will still be alive when my books have, like the Galaxy and Nature herself, passed away.

(CL 3, 733)

A heaven beyond imagining

TO MRS. JOHNSON   AUGUST 7, 1956

No, I don't wish I knew Heaven was like the picture in my *Great Divorce*, because, if we knew that, we should know it was no better. The good things even of this world are far too good ever to be reached by imagination. Even the common orange, you know: no one could have imagined it before he tasted it. How much less Heaven.

(CL 3, 778)

What does it mean to be "new creatures in Christ"?

TO STUART ROBERTSON　　　　　　　　MAY 6, 1962

On this point as on others the N[ew] T[estament] is highly paradoxical. St. Paul at the outset of an epistle sometimes talks as if the converts whom he is addressing were already wholly new creatures, already in the world of light, their old nature completely crucified. Yet by the end of the same epistle he will be warning the same people to avoid the very grossest vices.

Of himself he speaks sometimes as if his reward was perfectly sure: elsewhere he fears lest, having preached to others, he should be himself a castaway.

Our Lord Himself sometimes speaks as if all depended on faith, yet in the parable of the sheep and the goats all seems to depend on works: even works done or undone by those who had no idea what they were doing or undoing.

The best I can do about these mysteries is to think that the N.T. gives us a sort of double vision. A. Into our salvation as eternal fact, as it (and all else) is in the timeless vision of God. B. Into the same thing as a process worked out in time. Both must be true in some sense but it is beyond our capacity to envisage both together. Can one get a faint idea of it by thinking of A. A musical score as it is written down with all the notes there at once. B. The same thing *played* as a process in time? For *practical* purposes, however, it seems to me we must usually live by the second vision "working out our salvation in fear and trembling" (but it adds "for"—not "though"—but "for"—"it is God who worketh in us").

And in this temporal process surely God saves different souls in different ways? To preach instantaneous conversion and eternal security as if they must be the experiences of all who are saved, seems to me very dangerous: the very way to drive some into presumption and others into despair. How very different were the callings of the disciples.

I don't agree that if anyone were completely a new creature, you and I would necessarily recognize him as such. It takes holiness to detect holiness.

(CL 3, 1336–1337)

On the unforgivable sin

TO MR. GREEN   MAY 11, 1962

I also once ceased to believe and told others there is no God. In fact you and I both lost our faith and then returned to it. But surely we did not return on our own steam? Surely we were recalled by God? For no man can come, nor come back, to God unless God sends for him. The grace He has thus shown us for a second time is the proof that He has forgiven us. He has not cast us aside even though we, for a time, cast Him aside.

Don't forget that [John] Bunyan, as he himself tells us, thought that he had at one time committed the unforgivable sin. Yet he lived to write the *Pilgrim's Progress* and to be a great Christian champion.

It has always puzzled me very much that Our Lord should have told us there is an unforgivable sin and yet not told us what it is. [Matthew 12:31–32]. If it is a particular act which could be done at a particular time, the warning does not seem to be any use—like being told that there is a poisonous vegetable but not told which it is. But it may mean persistence in ordinary sin, a final refusal to repent or even to *try* to reform. If so, the warning would then be useful, a reminder that there is a point beyond which return becomes impossible. His purpose would be to fix the danger in our minds, but certainly *not* to set us looking through all our particular sins and trying to guess if some one of them was It.

As far as you (and I) are concerned I have no doubt that

the fear you mention is simply a temptation of the devil, an effort to keep us away from God by despair. It is often the devil working through some defect in our health, and in extreme cases it needs a medical as well as a spiritual cure. So don't listen to these fears and doubts* any more than you would to any obviously impure or uncharitable thoughts.

[Lewis's note] Of course, like other evil temptations, they will not be silenced at once. You will think you have got rid of them and then they will come back again—and again. But, with all our temptations of all sorts, we must just endure this. Keep on, do your duty, say your prayers, make your communions, and take no notice of the tempter. He goes away in the end. Remember I John 3:20 "If (= though) our heart condemn us, God is greater than our heart." Let us sometimes pray for one another.

(CL 3, 1340–1341)

A follow-up note to the same correspondent on the subject of the unforgivable sin

TO MR. GREEN   MAY 16, 1962

I was not only baptized in infancy, but, what seems to me far worse, I was already an apostate when I hypocritically allowed myself to be confirmed and made my first communion—in a state of total unbelief.

You'll find Bunyan's story (about how he thought he had committed the unforgivable sin) in *Grace Abounding to the Chief of Sinners*. I find also that our chaplain—a very good young man—once thought that he had done the same thing. He, by the way, took the view that those who had *really* done it would be the very last people to be bothered about it (in this life), for they would be hardened, which you—and, I dare to add, I—obviously are not.

There is a lovely passage in Pascal where he represents Our Lord as saying to the timorous soul "Be comforted. Unless you had found me, you would not be seeking me." God bless us both.

(CL 3, 1344)

On the resurrection of the body

TO MARY WILLIS SHELBURNE   NOVEMBER 26, 1962

My stuff about animals came long ago in *The Problem of Pain*. I ventured the supposal—it could be nothing more—that as we are raised *in* Christ, so at least some animals are raised *in* us. Who knows, indeed, but that a great deal even of the inanimate creation is raised *in* the redeemed souls who have, during this life, taken its beauty into themselves? That may be the way in which the "new heaven and the new earth" are formed. Of course we can only guess and wonder.

But these particular guesses arise in me, I trust, from taking seriously the resurrection of the body: a doctrine which nowadays is very soft pedaled by nearly all the faithful—to our great impoverishment. Not that you and I have now much reason to rejoice in having bodies! Like old automobiles, aren't they? where all sorts of apparently different things keep going wrong, but what they add up to is the plain fact that the machine is wearing out. Well, it was not meant to last forever. Still, I have a kindly feeling for the old rattle-trap. Through it God showed me that whole side of His beauty which is embodied in color, sound, smell and size. No doubt it has often led me astray: but not half so often, I suspect, as my soul has led *it* astray. For the spiritual evils which we share with the devils (pride, spite) are far worse than what we share with the beasts: and sensuality really arises more from the imagination than from the appetites; which, if left merely to their own animal strength, and not elaborated by our imagination, would be fairly easily managed. But this is turning into a sermon!

(CL 3, 1383–1384)

Questions About the Bible

C. S. LEWIS

On trying to read the Bible "devotionally"

TO DOM BEDE GRIFFITHS   APRIL 4, 1934

Devotion is best raised when we intend something else. At least that is my experience. Sit down to meditate devotionally on a single verse, and nothing happens. Hammer your way through a continued argument, just as you would in a profane writer, and the heart will sometimes sing unbidden.

(CL 2, 136)

Are all the books of the Bible equally historical?

TO CORBIN SCOTT CARNELL   APRIL 5, 1953

I am myself a little uneasy about the question you raise: there seems to be almost equal objection to the position taken up in my footnote and to the alternative of attributing the same kind and degree of historicity to all the books of the Bible. You see, the question about Jonah and the great fish does not turn simply on intrinsic probability. The point is that the whole *Book of Jonah* has to me the air of being a moral romance, a quite different *kind* of thing from, say, the account of King David or the New Testament narratives, not *pegged*, like them, into any historical situation.

In what sense does the Bible "present" this story "as historical"? Of course it doesn't *say* "This is fiction": but then neither does Our Lord *say* that His Unjust Judge, Good Samaritan, or Prodigal Son are fiction. (I would put *Esther* in the same category as Jonah for the same reason). How does a denial, or doubt, of their historicity lead logically to a similar denial of N.T. miracles?

Supposing (as I think is the case) that sound critical reading reveals different *kinds* of narrative in the Bible, surely it would be illogical to conclude that these different kinds should all be read in the same way? This is not a "rationalistic approach" to miracles. Where I doubt the historicity of an Old Testament narrative I never do so on the ground that the miraculous *as such* is incredible. Nor does it deny "a unique sort of inspiration": allegory, parable, romance, and lyric might be inspired as well as chronicle. I wish I could direct you to a good book on the subject, but I don't know one. With all good wishes.

(CL 3, 318–319)

On dealing with baffling passages in the Bible

TO MRS. EMILY MCLAY   AUGUST 8, 1953

Your experience in listening to those philosophers gives you the technique one needs for dealing with the dark places in the Bible. When one of the philosophers, one whom you know on other grounds to be a sane and decent man, said something you didn't understand, you did not at once conclude that he had gone off his head. You assumed you'd missed the point.

Same here. The two things one must NOT do are (a) To believe, on the strength of Scripture or on any other evidence, that God is in any way evil. (In Him is no *darkness* at all.*) (b) To wipe off the slate any passage which seems to show that He is. Behind that apparently shocking passage, be sure, there lurks some great truth which you don't understand. If one ever *does* come to understand it, one will see that [He] is good and just and gracious in ways we never dreamed of. Till then, it must be just left on one side.

But why are baffling passages left in at all? Oh because God speaks not only for us little ones but also to great sages and mystics who *experience* what we only *read about* and to whom all the words have therefore different (richer) contents. Would not a revelation which contained nothing that you and I did not understand, be for that very reason rather suspect? To a child it would seem a contradiction to say both that his parents made him and that God made him, yet we see both can be true.

*I John 1:5

(CL 3, 356–357)

On progressive revelation in the Bible

TO MRS. JOHNSON   MAY 14, 1955

My own view about Elisha and the bears* (not that I haven't known small boys who'd be much improved by the same treatment!) and other such episodes is something like this. If you take the Bible as a whole, you see a process in which something which, in its earliest levels (those aren't necessarily the ones that come first in the Book as now arranged) was hardly moral at all, and was in some ways not unlike the Pagan religions, is gradually purged and enlightened till it becomes the religion of the great prophets, and of Our Lord Himself. That whole process is the greatest revelation of God's true nature. At first hardly anything comes through but mere power. Then (very important) the truth that He is One and there is no other God. Then justice, then mercy, love, wisdom.

*2 Kings 2:23–24

(CL 3, 608)

On claims that Bible characters did not drink alcohol

TO MRS. JOHNSON   MAY 14, 1955

Of course Our Lord never drank *spirits* (they had no distilled liquors) but of course the wine of the Bible was real fermented wine and alcoholic. The repeated references to the sin of drunkenness in the Bible, from Noah's first discovery of wine* down to the warnings in St. Paul's epistles,** make this perfectly plain. The other theory could be (honestly) held only by a very ignorant person. One can understand the bitterness of some temperance fanatics if one had ever lived with a drunkard: what one finds it harder to excuse is any educated person telling such lies about history.

*Genesis 9:20–21

**Romans 13:13; Ephesians 5:18; 1 Timothy 3:3

(CL 3, 608)

The Bible as sacred history, but also as sacred myth and sacred fiction

TO JANET WISE   OCTOBER 5, 1955

My own position is not Fundamentalist, if Fundamentalism means accepting as a point of faith at the outset the proposition "Every statement in the Bible is completely true in the literal, historical sense." That would break down at once on the parables. All the same commonsense and general understanding of literary kinds which would forbid anyone to take the parables as historical statements, carried a very little further, would force us to distinguish between (1.) Books like *Acts* or the account of David's reign, which are everywhere dovetailed into a knowing history, geography, and genealogies (2.) Books like *Esther*, or *Jonah* or *Job* which deal with otherwise unknown characters living in unspecified periods, and pretty well *proclaim* themselves to be sacred fiction.

Such distinctions are not new. Calvin left the historicity of *Job* an open question and, from earlier, St. Jerome said that the whole Mosaic account of creation was done "after the method of a popular poet." Of course I believe the composition, presentation, and selection for inclusion in the Bible, of all the books to have been guided by the Holy Ghost. But I think He meant us to have sacred myth and sacred fiction as well as sacred history.

Mind you, I never think a story unhistorical *because* it is miraculous. I accept miracles. It's almost the manner that distinguishes the fiction from the histories. Compare the "Once upon a time" opening of *Job* with the accounts of David, St. Paul, or Our Lord Himself. The basis of our Faith is not the Bible taken by itself but the agreed affirmation of all Christendom: to which we owe the Bible itself.

(CL 3, 652–653)

C. S. LEWIS

In praise of the Psalms

TO MARY VAN DEUSEN   FEBRUARY 5, 1956

I am so glad you took to Psalm 36. My other great favorite is 19. First, the mere glory of nature (between the Psalms and Wordsworth—a long gap in history—you get nothing equal to either on this theme). Then the disinfectant, inexorable sun beating down on the desert and "nothing hid from the heat thereof." Then—implied, not stated—the imaginative identification of that heat and light with the "undefiled" law, the "clean" fear of the Lord, searching every cranny. Then the characteristically Jewish feeling that the Law is not only obligatory but beautiful, ravishing: delighting the heart, better than gold, sweeter than honey. Only after that, the (more Christian like) self-examination and humble petition. Nearly all that could be said before the Incarnation is said in this Psalm. It is so much *better Paganism* than the real Pagans* ever did! And in one way more glorious, more soaring and triumphant, than Christian poetry. For as God humbled Himself to become Man, so religion humbled itself to become Christianity.

*In Lewis's terminology, pre-Christian classical writers

(CL 3, 701)

What do we mean by the "inspiration" of Scripture?

TO LEE TURNER JULY 19, 1958

The main difficulty seems to me not the question *whether* the Bible is "inspired," but what exactly we mean by this. Our ancestors, I take it, believed that the Holy Spirit either just replaced the minds of the authors (like the supposed "control" in automatic writing) or at least dictated to them as to secretaries.

Scripture itself refutes these ideas. St. Paul distinguishes between what "the Lord" says and what he says "of himself"—yet *both* are "Scripture." Similarly the passages in which the prophets describe Theophanies and their own reactions to them would be absurd if they were not writing for themselves. Thus, without any modern scholarship, we are driven a long way from the extreme view of inspiration.

I myself think of it as analogous to the Incarnation—that, as in Christ a human soul-and-body are taken up and made the vehicle of Deity, so in Scripture, a mass of human legend, history, moral teaching etc. are taken up and made the vehicle of God's Word. Errors of minor fact are permitted to remain. (Was Our Lord Himself incapable, *qua* Man, of such errors? Would it be a real human incarnation if He was?)

One must remember of course that our modern and Western attention to dates, numbers, etc. simply did not exist in the ancient world. No one was looking for *that* sort of truth. . . . The blessed and significant thing is that none of all this has bothered your personal faith in Our Lord. Do you see clear reason why it need bother anyone else's?

(CL 3, 960–961)

Gentle Jesus meek and mild vs. the real Jesus

TO EDWARD LOFSTROM   JANUARY 16, 1959

"Gentle Jesus," my elbow! The most striking thing about Our Lord is the union of great ferocity with extreme tenderness. (Remember Pascal? "I do not admire the extreme of one virtue unless you show me at the same time the extreme of the opposite virtue. One shows one's greatness not by being at an extremity but by being simultaneously at two extremities *and filling all the space between*.")

Add to this that HE is also a supreme ironist, dialectician, and (occasionally) humorist. So go on! You are on the right track now: getting to the real Man behind all the plaster dolls that have been substituted for Him. This is the appearance in Human form of the God who made the Tiger *and* the Lamb, the avalanche *and* the rose. He'll frighten and puzzle you: but the real Christ *can* be loved and admired as the doll can't.

(CL 3, 1011)

To a correspondent who felt that Lewis's books challenged him more than reading the Bible

TO DON HOLMES   FEBRUARY 17, 1959

If my books are sometimes permitted by God to deliver to particular readers a more perceptible challenge than Scripture itself, I think this is because, in a sense, they catch people unprepared. We approach the Bible with reverence and with readiness to be edified. But by a curious and unhappy psychological law these attitudes often inhibit the very thing they are intended to facilitate. You see this in other things: many a couple never felt less in love than on their wedding day, many a man never felt less merry than at Christmas dinner, and when at a lecture we say "I *must* attend," attention instantly vanishes.

(CL 3, 1022–1023)

What is meant by the inspiration of Scripture?

TO CLYDE S. KILBY   MAY 7, 1959

(Clyde S. Kilby was a professor of English at Wheaton College in Illinois. Kilby sent Lewis a copy of the college's statement on the inspiration of Scripture and asked for Lewis's opinion. Kilby later began collecting Lewis's letters and papers, a collection now housed at the Marion E. Wade Center at Wheaton College.)

Thank you for your kind letter. I enclose what, at such short notice, I feel able to say on this question. If it is at all likely to upset anyone, throw it in the waste paper basket. Remember too that it is pretty tentative, much less an attempt to establish a view than a statement of the views on which, whether rightly or wrongly, I have come to work.

To me the curious thing is that neither in my own Bible-reading nor in my religious life as a whole does the question in fact even assume that importance which it always gets in theological controversy. The difference between reading the story of Ruth and that of Antigone—both first class as literature—is to me unmistakable and even overwhelming. But the question "Is Ruth historical?" (I've no reason to suppose it is not) doesn't really seem to arise till afterwards. It would still act on me as the Word of God if it weren't, so far as I can see. All Holy Scripture is written for our learning. But learning of what? I should have thought the value of some things (e.g. the Resurrection) depended on whether they really happened: but the value of others (e.g. the fate of Lot's wife) hardly at all. And the ones whose historicity matters are, as God's will, those where it is plain.

Whatever view we hold on the divine authority of Scripture must make room for the following facts

1. The distinction which St. Paul makes in I Cor. 7 between ἀλλὰ ο Κύριος (verse 10) and ἐγὼ λέγω, οὐκ ὁ Κύριος (verse 12).*
2. The apparent inconsistencies between the genealogies in Matt. 1 and Luke 3: between the accounts of the death of Judas in Matt. 27:5 and Acts 1:18–19.
3. St. Luke's own account of how he obtained his matter (1:1–4).
4. The universally admitted unhistoricity (I do not say, of course, falsity) of at least some narratives in Scripture (the parables), which may well extend also to Jonah and Job.
5. If every good and perfect gift comes from the Father of Lights then all true and edifying writings, whether in Scripture or not, must be in some sense inspired.
6. John 11:49–52. Inspiration may operate in a wicked man without his knowing it, and he can then utter the untruth he intends (propriety of making an innocent man a political scapegoat) as well as the truth he does not intend (the divine sacrifice).

It seems to me that 2 and 4 rule out the view that every statement in Scripture must be historical truth. And 1, 3, 5, and 6 rule out the view that inspiration is a single thing in the sense that, if present at all, it is always present in the same mode and the same degree. Therefore, I think, rule out the view that any one passage taken in isolation can be assumed to be inerrant in exactly the same sense as any other: e.g. that the numbers of O.T. armies (which in view of the size of the country, if true, involves continuous miracle) are statistically correct because the story of the Resurrection is historically correct. That the overall operation of Scripture is to convey God's Word to the reader (he also needs His inspiration) who reads it in the right spirit, I fully believe. That it also gives true answers to all the questions (often religiously irrelevant) which he might ask, I don't. The very kind of truth we are often demanding was, in my opinion, never even envisaged by the Ancients.

*1 Corinthians 7:10: "yet not I, but the Lord"; 1 Corinthians 7:12: "I say, not the Lord"

(CL 3, 1044–1045)

How could a good God command atrocities in the Old Testament?

TO JOHN BEVERSLUIS   JULY 3, 1963

On my view one must apply something of the same sort of explanation to, say, the atrocities (and treacheries) of Joshua.* I see the grave danger we run by doing so; but the danger of believing in a God whom we cannot but regard as evil, and then, in mere terrified flattery calling Him "good" and worshiping Him, is a still greater danger. The ultimate question is whether the doctrine of the goodness of God or that of the inerrancy of Scripture is to prevail when they conflict. I think the doctrine of the goodness of God is the more certain of the two. Indeed only that doctrine renders this worship of Him obligatory or even permissible.

To this some will reply "Ah, but we are fallen and don't recognize good when we see it." But God Himself does not say we are as fallen as all that. He constantly, in scripture, appeals to our conscience: "Why do ye not of *yourselves* judge what is right?"—"What fault hath my people found in Me?" And so on.

Socrates' answer to *Euthyphro* is used in Christian form by Hooker.** Things are not good because God commands them; God commands certain things because He sees them to be good. (In other words, the Divine will is the obedient servant of the Divine reason). The opposite view (Ockham's & Paley's)*** leads to the absurdity, if "good" means simply "what God wills" then to say "God is good" can mean only

"God wills what He wills." Which is equally true of you or me or Judas or Satan.

But of course having said all this, we must apply it with fear and trembling. Some things which seem to us bad may be good. But we must not corrupt our consciences by trying to feel a thing as good when it seems to us totally evil. We can only pray that *if* there is an invisible goodness hidden in such things, God, in His own good time will enable us to see it. If we need to. For perhaps sometimes God's answer might be "What is that to thee?" The passage may not be "addressed to our (your or my) condition" at all.

*Deuteronomy 7:1–2; 20:16–18

**In Plato's *Euthyphro*, Socrates asks, "Is piety loved by the gods because it is pious, or it is pious because it is loved by the gods?" Richard Hooker was a sixteenth-century English theologian.

***William of Ockham, fourteenth-century Franciscan philosopher; William Paley, eighteenth-century English clergyman

(CL 3, 1436–1437)

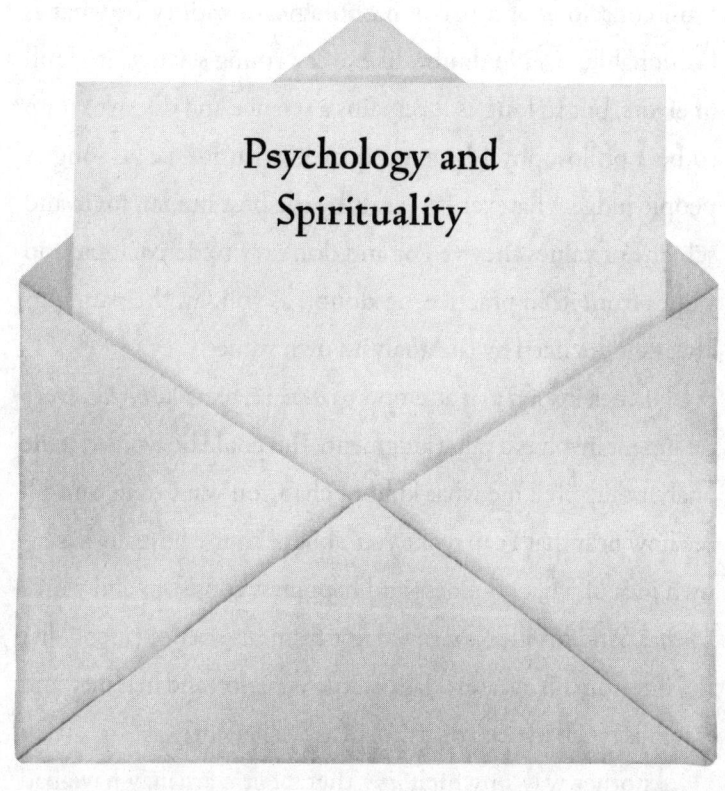

C. S. LEWIS

On psychoanalysis

TO MARY NEYLAN   MARCH 26, 1940

Psychoanalysis. In talking to me you must beware, because I am conscious of a partly pathological hostility to what is fashionable. . . . No doubt, like every young science, it is full of errors, but so long as it remains a science and doesn't set up to be a philosophy I have no quarrel with it—i.e. as long as people judge whatever it reveals by the best human logic and scheme of values they've got and don't try to derive logic and values from it. In practice, no doubt, as you say, the patient is always influenced by the analyst's own values.

Further, insofar as it attempts to *heal*, i.e. to make *better*, every treatment involves a value judgment. This could be avoided if the analyst said "Tell me what kind of chap you want to be and I'll see how near that I can make you": but of course he really has his own idea of what goodness and happiness consist in and works to that. And his idea is derived not from his science (it couldn't be) but from his age, sex, class, culture, religion and heredity, and is just as much in need of criticism as the patient's. . . .

Another way in which *any* therapeutic art may have bad philosophical results is this. It must, for the sake of method, take perfection as the Norm and treat every departure from it as disease: hence there is always a danger that those who practice it may come to treat a perfectly ideal perfection as "normal" in the popular sense and consequently waste their lives in crying for the moon.

(CL 2, 372–373)

Do agnostics still have a religion?

TO ELIZA MARIAN BUTLER   SEPTEMBER 25, 1940

A *pure* agnostic is a fine thing. I have known only one and he was the man who taught me to think. What I am worried about is the purity of your agnosticism: for one of the most dangerous things about the modern world seems to me the fact that most of those who call themselves agnostics have not really got rid of religion but merely exchanged civilized religion for barbarous religion—worship of sex, or the State, or the *élan vital*,* or the dead, or Mystery as such.

*Life Force philosophy of Henri Bergson

(CL 2, 444)

On the Shroud of Turin

TO SISTER PENELOPE   NOVEMBER 9, 1941

(who had sent Lewis an image of the head of the Shroud of Turin)

Thank you so much for the head of Our Lord from the shroud. It has grown upon me wonderfully. I don't commit myself to the genuineness. One can never be quite certain. But the great value is to make one realize that He was a man, and once even a dead man. There is so much difference between a doctrine and a realization.

(CL 2, 495)

Keep clear of psychiatrists who are not Christians

TO MRS. FRANK L. JONES　　　　　FEBRUARY 23, 1947

Keep clear of psychiatrists unless you know that they are also Christians. Otherwise they start with the assumption that your religion is an illusion and try to "cure" it: and this assumption they make not as professional psychologists but as amateur philosophers. Often they have never given the question any serious thought.

(CL 2, 765)

The dangers of introspection

TO "MRS. LOCKLEY"　　　　　SEPTEMBER 27, 1949

Yes, yes, I know. The moment one asks oneself "Do I believe?" all belief seems to go. I think this is because one is trying to turn round and look *at* something which is there to be used and work *from*—trying to take out one's eyes instead of keeping them in the right place and seeing *with* them. I find that it happens about other matters as well as faith. In my experience only very robust pleasures will stand the question, "Am I really enjoying this?" Or attention—the moment I begin thinking about my attention (to a book or a lecture) I have *ipso facto* [by the very fact] ceased attending. St. Paul speaks of "Faith actualized in Love." And "the heart is deceitful": you know better than I how very unreliable introspection is. I should be much more alarmed about your progress if you wrote claiming to be overflowing with Faith, Hope and Charity.

(CL 2, 983)

The danger of happiness and the benefit of unhappiness

TO "MRS. LOCKLEY"   MARCH 5, 1951

The great thing is to stop thinking about happiness. Indeed the best thing about happiness itself is that it liberates you from thinking about happiness—as the greatest pleasure that money can give us is to make it unnecessary to think about money. And one sees why we have to be taught the "not thinking" when we lack as well as when we have. And I'm sure that, as you say, you will "get through somehow in the end."

Here is one of the fruits of unhappiness: that it forces us to think of life as something to go *through*. And out at the other end. If only we could steadfastly do that while we are happy, I suppose we should need no misfortunes. It is hard on God really. To how few of us He *dare* send happiness because He knows we will forget Him if He gave us any sort of nice things for the moment...

(CL 3, 93)

Grace is not frustrated by doubts

TO "MRS. LOCKLEY"   MARCH 5, 1951

I *do* get that sudden feeling that the whole thing [Christian faith] is hocus pocus and it now worries me hardly at all. Surely the mechanism is quite simple? Skeptical, incredulous, materialistic *ruts* have been deeply engraved in our thought, perhaps even in our physical brains by all of our earlier lives. At the slightest jerk our thought will flow down those old ruts. And notice when the jerks come. Usually at the precise moment when we might receive Grace. And if you were a devil would you not give the jerk just at those moments? I think that all Christians have found that he is very active near the altar or on the eve of conversion: worldly anxieties, physical discomforts, lascivious fancies, doubt, are often poured in at such junctures . . . But the Grace is not frustrated. One gets *more* by pressing steadily on through these interruptions than on occasions when all goes smoothly . . .

(CL 3, 93)

On the vastness and the smallness of the soul

TO WARFIELD M. FIROR   MARCH 27, 1951

The whole difficulty with me is to keep control of the mind and I wish one's earliest education had given one more training in that. There seems to be a disproportion between the vastness of the soul in one respect (i.e. as a mass of ideas and emotions) and its smallness in another (i.e. as central, controlling ego). The whole inner weather changes so complete in less than a minute. Do you read George Herbert—

If what my soul doth feel sometimes
My soul might always feel—

(CL 3, 105)

Forgiving oneself

TO MISS BRECKENRIDGE   APRIL 19, 1951

I think that if God forgives us we must forgive ourselves. Otherwise it is almost like setting up ourselves as a higher tribunal than Him.

(CL 3, 109)

On the subjectivity of psychiatry

TO MARY VAN DEUSEN   JUNE 10, 1952

I think psychiatry is like surgery: i.e. the thing is in itself essentially an infliction of wounds but may, in good hands, be necessary to avoid some greater evil. But it is more tricky than surgery because the personal philosophy and character of the operator come more into play. In setting a broken ankle all surgeons would agree as to the proper position to which the bones should be restored, because anatomy is an exact science. But all psychiatrists are not agreed as to the proper shape of the soul: where their ideas of that proper shape are based on a heathen or materialistic philosophy, they may be aiming at a shape *we* should strongly disapprove. One wants a Christian psychiatrist. There are a few of these, but nothing like enough.

(CL 3, 200)

Does God seem real?

TO MRS. JOHNSON JULY 17, 1953

"Does God seem real to me?" It varies: just as lots of other things I firmly believe in (my own death, the solar system) *feel* more or less real at different times. I have dreamed dreams but not seen visions: but don't think all that matters a hoot. And the saints say that visions are unimportant. If Our Lord *did* seem to appear to you at your prayer (bodily) what after all could you do but go on with your prayers? How could you know that it was not a hallucination?

(CL 3, 348)

Constancy of faith amid fleeting feelings

TO MARY VAN DEUSEN JULY 23, 1953

It is a great joy to be able to "feel" God's love as a reality, and one must give thanks for it and use it. But you must be prepared for the feeling dying away again, for feelings are by nature impermanent. The great thing is to continue to believe when the feeling is absent: and these periods do quite as much for one as those when the feeling is present.

(CL 3, 350–351)

Letters to Roman Catholics and About Catholic Doctrines

On avoiding arguments between Christian denominations

TO DOM BEDE GRIFFITHS   APRIL 4, 1934

I had better say once and for all that I do not intend to discuss with you in future, if I can help it, any of the questions at issue between our respective churches [Roman Catholic and Anglican] ... I do not think there is anything distressing for either of us in agreeing to be silent on this matter: I have had a Catholic among my most intimate friends for many years [J. R. R. Tolkien] and a great deal of our conversation has been religious. When all is said (and truly said) about the divisions of Christendom, there remains, by God's mercy, an enormous common ground. It is abstaining from one tree in the whole garden.

(CL 2, 135–136)

Why Lewis was not a Roman Catholic

TO H. LYMAN STEBBINS   MAY 8, 1945

My position about the Churches can best be made plain by an imaginary example. Suppose I want to find out the correct interpretation of Plato's teaching. What I am most confident in accepting is that interpretation which is common to all the

Platonists down all the centuries: what Aristotle and the Renaissance scholars and Paul Elmer More* agree on I take to be true Platonism. Any purely modern views which claim to have discovered for the first time what Plato meant, and say that everyone from Aristotle down has misunderstood him, I reject out of hand.

But there is something else I would also reject. If there were an ancient Platonic Society still existing at Athens and claiming to be the exclusive trustees of Plato's meaning, I should approach them with great respect. But if I found that their teaching in many ways was curiously unlike the actual text and unlike what ancient interpreters said, and in some cases could not be traced back to within 1,000 years of his time, I should reject these exclusive claims: while still ready, of course, to take any particular thing they taught on its merits.

I do the same with Christianity. What is most certain is the vast mass of doctrine which I find agreed on by Scripture, the Fathers, the Middle Ages, modern Roman Catholics, modern Protestants. That is true "catholic" doctrine. Mere "modernism" I reject at once.**

The Roman Church where it differs from this universal tradition and specially from apostolic Christianity I reject. Thus their theology about the B.V.M.*** I reject because it seems utterly foreign to the New Testament where indeed the words "Blessed is the womb that bore thee" receive a rejoinder pointing in exactly the opposite direction. Their papalism seems equally foreign to the attitude of St. Paul towards St. Peter in the Epistles. The doctrine of Transubstantiation insists in defining in a way which the New Testament seems to me not to countenance. In a word, the whole setup of modern Romanism seems to me to be as much a provincial or local *variation* from the central, ancient tradition as any particular Protestant sect is. I must therefore reject their *claim*: though this does not mean rejecting particular things they say.

I'm afraid I haven't read any modern books of Roman-Anglican controversy. Hooker (*Laws of Ecclesiastical Polity*) is to me the great formulation of Anglicanism. But the great point is that in one sense there's no such thing as Anglicanism. What we are committed to believing is whatever can be proved from Scripture. On that subject there is room for endless progress. However you decide, good wishes. Mention me in your prayers.

*American critic and essayist

**"Modernism" refers to contemporary approaches to Christian faith that eliminate miracles and supernatural elements.

***Blessed Virgin Mary

(CL 2, 645–647)

Letters in Latin to Don Giovanni Calabria

(The following are excerpts from the many letters Lewis composed in Latin to Don Giovanni Calabria, an Italian priest and founder of the Congregation of the Poor Servants of Divine Providence. Don Giovanni did not speak English, so the two corresponded in Latin.)

September 6, 1947
Reverend Father,

Thank you for your letter, full of love and goodwill. Be assured that for me too the schism in the Body of Christ is both a source of grief and a matter for prayers, being a most serious stumbling block to those coming in and one which makes even the faithful weaker in repelling the common foe. However, I am a layman, indeed the most lay of laymen, and least skilled in the deeper questions of sacred theology. I have tried to do the only thing that I think myself able to do: that is, to leave completely aside the subtler questions about which the Roman Church and Protestants disagree among themselves—things which are to be treated by bishops and learned men—and in my own books to expound, rather, those things which still, by God's grace, after so many sins and errors, are shared by us. Nor is this a pointless task; for I find that people are unaware how many matters we even now agree on—so much so that I have come across someone who believed that you deny the Three in One God! Over and above that work, it has always seemed to me that I should maintain as much fraternal intercourse as possible with all those who call themselves Christians. If all were actively to do this, might we not hope that this unity of love and action over many years would precede—not to say foster—an eventual reunification of doctrines. Thirdly, there remain—what is most efficacious—prayers.

The practice of writing in Latin is one which for many years I have not kept up! If I have committed any solecism, I ask pardon.

Let us pray for each other. With all my heart I commend myself to your fatherly love in Our Lord.

(CL 2, 801)

September 20, 1947
Reverend Father,

I was glad to receive your further letter written on the 15th Sept. The hour, as you say, is indeed Satan's hour. But I see some sparks of hope in the darkness.

Common perils, common burdens, an almost universal hatred and contempt for the Flock of Christ can, by God's Grace, contribute much to the healing of our divisions. For those who suffer the same things from the same people for the same Person can scarcely not love each other.

Indeed I could well believe that it is God's intention, since we have refused milder remedies, to compel us into unity, by persecution even and hardship. Satan is without doubt nothing else than a hammer in the hand of a benevolent and severe God. For all, either willingly or unwillingly, do the will of God: Judas and Satan as tools or instruments, John and Peter as sons.

Even now we see more charity, or certainly less hatred, between separated Christians than there was a century ago. The chief cause of this (under God) seems to me to be the swelling pride and barbarity of the unbelievers. Hitler, unknowingly and unwillingly, greatly benefited the Church!

(CL 2, 804)

December 26, 1951

Dearest Father,

Thank you for the letter which I have received from

you today and I invoke upon you all spiritual and temporal blessings in the Lord.

As for myself, during the past year a great joy has befallen me. Difficult though it is, I shall try to explain this in words. It is astonishing that sometimes we believe that we believe what, really, in our heart, we do not believe.

For a long time I believed that I believed in the forgiveness of sins. But suddenly (on St. Mark's day) this truth appeared in my mind in so clear a light that I perceived that never before (and that after many confessions and absolutions) had I believed it with my whole heart.

So great is the difference between mere affirmation by the intellect and that faith, fixed in the very marrow and as it were palpable, which the Apostle wrote was *substance*.

Perhaps I was granted this deliverance in response to your intercessions on my behalf!

This emboldens me to say to you something that a layman ought scarcely to say to a priest nor a junior to a senior. (On the other hand, *out of the mouths of babes*: indeed, as once to Balaam, out of the mouth of an ass!) It is this: you write much about your own sins. Beware (permit me, my dearest Father, to say beware) lest humility should pass over into anxiety or sadness. It is bidden us to "rejoice and always rejoice". Jesus has cancelled the handwriting which was against us. Lift up our hearts!

Permit me, I pray you, these stammerings. You are ever in my prayers and ever will be.

Farewell.

(CL 3, 151–152)

July 14, 1952

Thank you, dearest Father, both for the tracts of your Congregation and for your letter dated July 7th.

The times we live in are, as you say, grave: whether "graver than all others in history" I do not know. But the evil that is closest always seems to be the most serious: for as with the eye so with the heart, it is a matter of one's own perspective. However, if our times are indeed the worst, if That Day is indeed now approaching, what remains but that we should rejoice because our redemption is now nearer and say with St. John: "Amen; come quickly, Lord Jesus."

Meanwhile our only security is that The Day may find us working each one in his own station and especially (giving up dissensions) fulfilling that supreme command that we love one another.

Let us ever pray for each other.

Farewell: and may there abide with you and me that peace which no one can take from us.

(CL 3, 214)

March 17, 1953

My dearest Father,

I was delighted, as always, by your letter.

It is a wonderful thing and a strengthening of faith that two souls differing from each other in place, nationality, language, obedience and age should have been thus led into a delightful friendship; so far does the order of spiritual beings transcend the material order.

It makes easier that necessary doctrine that we are most closely joined together alike with the sinner Adam and with the Just One, Jesus, even though as to body, time and place we have lived so differently from both. This unity of the whole human race exists: would that there existed that nobler union of which you write. No day do I let pass without my praying for that longed-for consummation.

What you say about the present state of mankind is true: indeed, it is even worse than you say.

For they neglect not only the law of Christ but even the Law of Nature as known by the Pagans. For now they do not blush at adultery, treachery, perjury, theft and the other crimes which I will not say Christian Doctors, but the Pagans and the Barbarians have themselves denounced.

They err who say "the world is turning pagan again." Would that it were! The truth is that we are falling into a much worse state.

"Post-Christian man" is not the same as "pre-Christian man." He is as far removed as virgin is from widow: there is nothing in common except want of a spouse: but there is a great difference between a spouse-to-come and a spouse lost.

(CL 3, 306–307)

August 10, 1953
Dearest Father,

I have received your letter dated the 5th August. I await with gratitude the pamphlets—a specimen of your people's printing skill: which however I shall not see for 5 weeks because tomorrow I am crossing over (if God so have pleased) to Ireland: my birthplace and dearest refuge so far as charm of landscape goes, and temperate climate, although most dreadful because of the strife, hatred and often civil war between dissenting faiths.

There indeed both yours and ours "know not by what Spirit they are led." They take lack of charity for zeal and mutual ignorance for orthodoxy.

I think almost all the crimes which Christians have perpetrated against each other arise from this, that religion is confused with politics. For, above all other spheres of human life, the Devil claims politics for his own, as almost the citadel of his power. Let us, however, with mutual prayers pray with all our power for that charity which "covers a multitude of sins." Farewell, comrade and father.

(CL 3, 358)

On Avoiding Arguments by Letter

TO SISTER MARY ROSE   JANUARY 1950

I am sorry if I misunderstood your letter: and I think that you misunderstood mine. What I meant was that if I replied to your original question (why I am not a member of the Roman Church) I should have to write a very long letter. It would of course be answerable: and your answer would be answerable by me . . . and so on. The resulting correspondence would certainly not, of course, be in excess of the importance of the subject: but haven't you and I both probably more pressing duties? For a real correspondence on such a subject would be nearly a whole-time job. I thought we could both discuss the matter more usefully with people nearer at hand. Even the two letters which we have exchanged have already revealed the pitfalls of argument by letter. With all good wishes.

(CL 3, 8–9)

Avoiding discussions which endanger charity

TO MRS. HALMBACHERMARCH 1951

The question for me (naturally) is not "Why should I not be a Roman Catholic?" but "Why should I?" But I don't like discussing such matters, because it emphasizes differences and endangers charity. By the time I had really explained my objection to certain doctrines which differentiate you from us (and also in my opinion from the Apostolic and even the Medieval Church), you would like me less.

(CL 3, 106)

On saluting the Blessed Virgin Mary

TO MARY VAN DEUSENJUNE 26, 1952

Incense and Hail Marys are in quite different categories. The one is merely a question of ritual: some find it helpful and others don't, and each must put up with its absence or presence in the church they are attending with cheerful and charitable humility.

But Hail Marys raise a *doctrinal* question: whether it is lawful to address devotions to any *creature*, however holy. My own view would be that a *salute* to any saint (or angel) cannot in itself be wrong any more than taking off one's hat to a friend: but that there is always some danger lest such practices start one on the road to a state (sometimes found in R.C.'s [Roman Catholics]) where the B.V.M. [Blessed Virgin Mary] is treated really as a deity and even becomes the center of the religion. I therefore think that such salutes are better avoided. And if the Blessed Virgin is as good as the best mothers I have known, she does not *want* any of the attention which might have gone to her Son diverted to herself.

(CL 3, 209)

The existence of purgatory as private speculation, not required doctrine

TO MR. ALLCOCK MARCH 24, 1955

The doctrine of purgation after death is one of the many held by the Roman Church which I consider to be intrinsically probable but which, since it is not clearly stated in Scripture, nor included in the early creeds, I do not think they have any warrant for enforcing. I repudiate their practice of defining and systematizing and continually enumerating the list of things that *must* be accepted. But that is quite consistent with my believing, as private speculations, some of the things they accept as revealed certainties. For of course one may "assert" (in the sense "hold as private opinion") lots that one does not "believe" in the sense of holding as faith. E.g. I personally on general historical grounds may "believe" that our Lord could speak a certain amount of Greek . . . ?

I'd be a wicked idiot if I went about putting this forward as an article of faith: nor would it make the slightest difference to my religious life if I found my opinion to be wrong. A similar distinction is quite familiar to us in another field. You accept certain statements (e.g. that water is H_2O) as scientific certainties: but you probably "believe" a good many other things about the physical world you would admit to be only probable and, if you were a teacher, would not at all object to your pupil's denying.

(CL 3, 587–588)

Confessions About His Own Struggles

Struggling with chronic temptations

TO MARY NEYLAN   JANUARY 20, 1942

I know all about the despair of overcoming chronic temptations. It is not serious provided self-offended petulance, annoyance at breaking records, impatience etc. doesn't get the upper hand. No *amount* of falls will really undo us if we keep on picking ourselves up each time. We shall of course be very muddy and tattered children by the time we reach home. But the bathrooms are all ready, the towels put out, and the clean clothes are in the airing cupboard. The only fatal thing is to lose one's temper and give it up. It is when we notice the dirt that God is most present to us: it is the very sign of His presence.

(CL 2, 507)

A poem on his self-doubts as a Christian apologist

(An apologist is one who offers a defense of the faith)

TO SISTER PENELOPE   JULY 29, 1942

As for my "special needs," which you kindly ask for, this "Apologist's Evening Hymn" I've just completed, will tell you.

From all my lame defeats and oh! much more
From all the victories I have seemed to score;
From cleverness shot forth in Thy behalf,
At which, while angels weep, the audience laugh;
From all my proofs of Thy divinity,
Thou, who would'st give no sign, deliver me.
Thoughts are but coins. Let me not trust, instead
Of Thee, the thumb-worn image of Thy head;
From every thought, even from my thoughts of Thee,
Oh thou fair Silence! fall and set me free.
Lord of the straight way and the needle's eye,
Take from me all my trumpery lest I die.

(CL 2, 527)

On interruptions of one's "real life"

TO ARTHUR GREEVES   DECEMBER 20, 1943

The great thing, if one can, is to stop regarding all the unpleasant things as interruptions of one's "own," or "real" life. The truth is of course that what one calls the interruptions are precisely one's real life—the life God is sending one day by day: what one calls one's "real life" is a phantom of one's own imagination. This at least is what I see at moments of insight: but it's hard to remember it all the time . . .

Isn't it hard to *go on* being patient, to go on supplying sympathy?

(CL 2, 595)

The rule of the universe is doing for others

TO ARTHUR GREEVES   JULY 2, 1949

Thanks for your most kind and comforting letter—like a touch of a friend's hand in a dark place. [Lewis continues by recounting his brother Warren's struggles with alcohol abuse.]

Don't imagine I doubt for a moment that what God sends us must be sent in love and will all be for the best if we have grace to use it so. My *mind* doesn't waver on that point: my *feelings* sometimes do. That's why it does me good to hear what I believe repeated in your voice—it being the rule of the universe that others can do for us what we cannot do for ourselves and one can paddle every canoe *except* one's own. That is why Christ's suffering *for us* is not a mere theological dodge but the supreme case of the law that governs the whole world: and when they mocked him by saying "He saved others, himself he cannot save"* they were really uttering, little as they knew it, the ultimate law of the spiritual world.

*Matthew 27:42

(CL 2, 952–953)

What right have I to expect the peace of God?

TO WARFIELD M. FIROR   DECEMBER 5, 1949

I am concerned about that at present, chiefly as a result of reading William Law.* It's all there in the New Testament, though. "Dying to the world"—"The world is crucified to me and I to the world." And I find I haven't begun: at least not if it means (and can it mean less than) a steady and progressive disentangling of all one's motives from the merely natural or this-worldly objects: like training a creeper to grow up one wall instead of another. I don't mean disentangling from things wrong in themselves, but, say, from the very pleasant evening which we hope to have over one of your hams tomorrow night,** or from gratification at my literary success. It is not the things, nor even the pleasure in them, but the fact that in such pleasures my heart, or so much of my heart, lies. Or to put it in a fantastic form—if a voice said to me (and one I couldn't disbelieve) "you shall never see the face of God, never help to save a neighbor's soul, never be free from sin, but you shall live in perfect health till the age of 100, very rich, and die the most famous man in the world, and pass into a twilight consciousness of a vaguely pleasant sort forever"—how much would it worry me? How much compared with another war? Or even with an announcement that I should have to have all my teeth out? You see? And what right have I to expect the Peace of God while I thus put my whole heart, at least all my strongest wishes, in the world which he has warned me against?

Well, thank God (for there is still part of me, a tiny little infantine voice somewhere amidst all the strong, confident *natural* voices, which can just thank Him, or perhaps only thank Him for being able to wish to thank Him) we shall not be left to the world. All His terrible resources (but it is we who force him to use them) will be brought against us to detach us from it—insecurity, war, poverty, pain, unpopularity, loneliness. We must be taught that this tent is not home. And, by Jove, how terrible it would be if all suffering, including death itself, were *optional*, so that only a very few voluntary ascetics ever even attempted to achieve the end for which we are created. *A propos*—dare we gloss the text "Strait is the way and few there be that find it"*** by adding "And that's why most of you have to be bustled and badgered into it like sheep—and the sheepdogs have to have pretty sharp teeth too!" I hope so.

*William Law: author of *A Serious Call to a Devout and Holy Life* (1729)

**The correspondent was an American admirer of Lewis who often sent him hams and other gifts.

***Matthew 7:13–14

(CL 2, 1007–1008)

On feeling he would outlive his literary fame

TO WARFIELD M. FIROR   DECEMBER 20, 1951

I am going to be (if I live long enough) one of those men who *was* a famous writer in his forties and dies unknown—like Christian [in *Pilgrim's Progress*] going down into the green valley of humiliation. Which is the most beautiful thing in Bunyan and can be the most beautiful thing in life if a man takes it *quite* rightly—a matter I think and pray about a good deal. One thing is certain: much better to begin (at least) learning humility on this side of the grave than to have it all as a fresh problem on the other. Anyway, the desire which has to be mortified is such a vulgar and silly one.

(CL 3, 150)

Dealing with estrangement from one's father

TO RHONA BODLE   MARCH 24, 1954

Oh how you touch my conscience! I treated my own father abominably and no sin in my whole life now seems to be so serious. . . .

Feelings of affection are not at the command of the will and perhaps the very attempt to produce them has the opposite effect. I have been astonished at the ease (and even the affection) with which I have been able to treat in *other* old men the very same characteristics I was so impatient with in my Father. I wonder can something be done along those lines?—by remembering how merely funny, how endearing in a whimsical way, the things that divide you from your Father would seem if he were a casual acquaintance. By voluntarily standing further off might one in effect come closer? Part of the difficulty, I fancy, is heredity—a deep awareness that what one likes least in our parents has been bequeathed to oneself and, in oneself, needs to be resisted. While my Father was alive I was shocked when I caught myself acting or speaking like him: now I am amused, and not hostilely. At any rate, work now for the night cometh.*

*John 9:4

(CL 3, 445)

Momentary joy that transfigures the past

TO PHYLLIS ELINOR SANDEMAN   DECEMBER 11, 1952

(Author of *Treasure on Earth*, a memoir about spending Christmas in her childhood at Lyme Park, the family country estate.)

You will notice when you reread your book in a different mood that it doesn't really give the impression of a very happy childhood. Ecstatic, yes: shot through with raptures and tingling delights, but not very secure, not very consoled. And that, I believe, is absolutely true: I fancy *happy* childhoods are usually forgotten. It is not settled comfort and heartsease but momentary joy that transfigures the past and lets the eternal quality show through. (I sometimes eat parsnips because their taste, which I dislike, reminds me of my prep-school, which I disliked: but those two dislikes don't in the least impair the strange joy of "being reminded.")

(CL 3, 263)

Equally hard to believe and to disbelieve in the afterlife

TO PHYLLIS ELINOR SANDEMAN   DECEMBER 11, 1952

Yes, people do find it hard to keep on feeling as if you believed in the next life: but then it is just as hard to keep on feeling as if you believed you were going to be nothing after death. I know this because in the old days before I was a Christian I used to try.

(CL 3, 744–745)

The pitfalls of constantly defending one's faith

TO MARY VAN DEUSEN   JUNE 18, 1956

I envy you not having to think any more about Christian apologetics. My correspondents force the subject on me again and again. It is very wearing, and not very good for one's own faith. A Christian doctrine never seems less real to me than when I have just (even if successfully) been defending it.

(CL 3, 762)

Questions About Narnia

Aslan's name in our world

TO HILA NEWMAN   JUNE 3, 1953

As to Aslan's other name, well I want you to guess. Has there never been anyone in *this* world who (1.) Arrived at the same time as Father Christmas. (2.) Said he was the son of the Great Emperor. (3.) Gave himself up for someone else's fault to be jeered at and killed by wicked people. (4.) Came to life again. (5.) Is sometimes spoken of as a Lamb (see the end of the Dawn Treader). Don't you really know His name in this world. Think it over and let me know your answer!

(CL 3, 334)

Why characters in the Narnia books can be grown-ups in Narnia while remaining children on earth

TO PHYLLIDA   SEPTEMBER 14, 1953

I don't think age matters so much as people think. Parts of me are still 12 and I think other parts were already 50 when I was 12: so I don't feel it very odd that they grow up in Narnia while they are children in England.

(CL 3, 362)

To a mother whose six-year-old son, Laurence, worried that he loved Aslan more than he did Jesus

TO PHILINDA KRIEG   MAY 6, 1955

Tell Laurence from me, with my love:

1. Even if he was loving Aslan more than Jesus (I'll explain in a moment why he can't really be doing this) he would not be an idol-worshiper. If he was an idol-worshiper he'd be doing it on purpose, whereas he's now doing it because he can't help doing it, and trying hard not to do it. But God knows quite well how hard we find it to love Him more than anyone or anything else, and He won't be angry with us as long as we are trying. And He will help us.
2. But Laurence can't *really* love Aslan more than Jesus, even if he feels that's what he is doing. For the things he loves Aslan for doing or saying are simply the things Jesus really did and said. So that when Laurence thinks he is loving Aslan, he is really loving Jesus: and perhaps loving Him more than he ever did before. Of course there is one thing Aslan has that Jesus has not—I mean, the body of a lion. (But remember, if there are other worlds and they need to be saved and Christ were to save them as He would—He may really have taken all sorts of bodies in them which we don't know about.)

Now if Laurence is bothered because he finds the lion-body seems nicer to him than the man-body, I don't think he need be bothered at all. God knows all about the way a little boy's imagination works (He made it, after all) and knows that at a certain age the idea of talking and friendly animals is very attractive. So I don't think He minds if Laurence likes the Lion-body. And anyway, Laurence will find as he grows older, that feeling (liking the lion-body better) will die away of itself, without his taking any trouble about it. So he needn't bother.

3. If I were Laurence I'd just say in my prayers something like this: "Dear God, if the things I've been thinking and feeling about those books are things You don't like and are bad for me, please take away those feelings and thoughts. But if they are not bad, then please stop me from worrying about them. And help me every day to love you more in the way that really matters far more than any feelings or imaginations, by doing what you want and growing more like you." That is the sort of thing I think Laurence should say for himself; but it would be kind and Christian-like if he then added, "And if Mr. Lewis has worried any other children by his books or done them any harm, then please forgive him and help him never to do it again."

Will this help? I am terribly sorry to have caused such trouble, and would take it as a great favor if you would write again and tell me how Laurence goes on. I shall of course have him daily in my prayers. He must be a corker of a boy: I hope you are prepared for the possibility he might turn out a saint. I daresay the saints' mothers have, in some ways, a rough time!

(CL 3, 602–603)

On Sorrow and Death, Consolation and Courage

C. S. LEWIS

Misguided efforts to cancel death

TO MRS. PERCIVAL WISEMAN   MARCH 20, 1944

You are quite right to keep clear of the Spiritualists. All that is an effort to *cancel* death, to go on getting a pale phantom of the same sort of intercourse with our dear ones which we had when they and we were members of the same world. But we must *submit* to death, embrace the cross.

I think the purpose of the separation is to help us to turn what is merely natural and instinctive affection into real spiritual love of them in Christ. Not that natural affection isn't good and innocent, but it is merely natural—and therefore must first be crucified before it can rise again. Those who try to escape the crucifixion fall in either with charlatans or with delusions from hell: spiritualism often drives people mad. Of course, we should pray for our dead as I'm sure they do for us.

(CL 2, 607–608)

On the death of his friend Charles Williams

TO ANNE RIDLER   JUNE 3, 1945

It is an interesting fact that everyone almost who has spoken or written to me about his death says something different of him and all true. One feels curiously *un*-depressed, do you find? It has increased enormously one's faith in the next life and I can't help feeling him all over the place. I can't put it into words: I never knew the death of a good man could itself do so much good. I don't mean there isn't pain, pain in plenty: but not dull, sullen, sickening, drab, resentful pain.

(CL 2, 659)

The newly dead may have the power to bless those they have left behind

TO VERA MATHEWS   MARCH 27, 1951

I have just got your letter of the 22nd containing the sad news of your father's death. But, dear lady, I hope you and your mother are not really "trying to pretend it didn't happen." It does happen, happens to all of us, and I have no patience with the high minded people who make out that it "doesn't matter." It matters a great deal, and very solemnly. And for those who are left, the pain is not the whole thing. I feel very strongly (and I am not alone in this) that some good comes from the dead to the living in the months or weeks after the death. I think I was much helped by my own father after his death: as if our Lord welcomed the newly dead with the gift of some power to bless those they have left behind;

His *birthday* present. Certainly, they often seem just at that time, to be very near us. God bless you all and give you grace to receive all the good in this, as in every other event, that is intended you.

(CL 3, 103–104)

Comments to a friend who had recently lost her husband

TO PHYLLIS ELINOR SANDEMAN   DECEMBER 22, 1953

First, you may be quite sure that I realize (I'd be a fool if I didn't) that there is something in a loss like yours which no unmarried person can understand. Secondly, that nothing I or anyone can say will remove the *pain*. There are no anesthetics. About the bewilderment and about the right and wrong ways of using the pain, something may perhaps be done: but one can't stop it hurting. The *worst* way of using the pain, you have already avoided: i.e. resentment.

Now about not wanting to pray, surely there is one person you very much want to pray for: your husband himself. You ask, can he help you, but isn't this probably the time for you to help him. In one way, you see, you are further on than he: you had begun to know God. He couldn't help you in *that* way: it seems to me quite possible that you can now help more than while he was alive. So get on with that right away. Our Lord said that man and wife were one flesh and forbade any man to put them asunder: and we may be sure He doesn't do Himself what He forbade us to do. Your present prayers for your husband are still part of the married life.

Then as for your own shock in discovering that you hadn't got nearly as far as you thought towards loving the God who made your husband and gave him to you more than the gift. Well, no. One keeps on thinking one has crossed that bridge before one has. And God knows that it has to be crossed sooner or later, in this life or in another. And the first step is to discover that one has *not* crossed it yet. I wonder could He have really shown you this in any other way? Or even if we can't answer that, can't we trust Him to know *when* and *how* best the terrible operation can be done? Of course it is easy (I know) for the person who isn't feeling the pain to say all these things. You yourself would have been able to say them of anyone else's loss. Whatever *rational* grounds there are for doubt, you knew them all before: can it be rational (of course, it is *natural*) to weight them so differently simply because, this time, oneself is the sufferer? Doesn't that make it obvious that the doubts come not from the reason but from the shrinking nerves? At any rate, don't try to argue with them: not now, while you are crippled. Ignore them: go on. Be regular in all your religious duties. Remember it is not being loved but loving which is the high and holy thing. You are now practicing the second without the full comfort of the first. It was certain from the beginning that you would some day have to do this, for no human love passes onto the eternal level in any other way.

(CL 3, 392–393)

To a newly bereaved correspondent

TO MRS. D. JESSUP   JANUARY 5, 1954

Oh I am sorry. How dreadful....

I don't know whether anything an outsider can say is much use; and you know already the things we have been taught—that suffering *can* (but oh!, with what difficulty) be offered to God as our part in the whole redemptive suffering of the world beginning with Christ's own suffering: that suffering by itself does not fester or poison, but resentment does; that sufferings which (heaven knows) fell on us without and against our will can be so taken that they are as saving and purifying as the voluntary sufferings of martyrs & ascetics.

And it *is* all true, and it is so hard to go on believing it. Especially as the dark time in which you are now entering (I've tried it; my own life really begins with my Mother's illness and death from cancer when I was about 9) is split up into so many minor horrors and fears and upsets, some of them trivial and prosaic.

May God support you. Keep a firm hold of the Cross. And try to keep clear of the modern fancy that all this is abnormal and that you have been singled out for something outrageous. For no one escapes. We are all driven into the front line to be sorted sooner or later. With all blessings and with deep sorrow.

(CL 3, 404–405)

God may be most present when we feel his presence least

TO MARY MARGARET MCCASLIN   AUGUST 2, 1954

I will certainly put you in my prayers. I can well believe that you were divinely supported at the time of your terrible calamity. People often are. It is afterwards, when the new and bleaker life is beginning to be a routine, that one often feels one has been left rather unaided. I am sure one is not really so. God's presence is not the same as the feeling of God's presence and He may be doing most for us when we think He is doing least.

Loneliness, I am pretty sure, is one of the ways by which we can grow spiritually. Until we are lonely we may easily think we have got further than we really have in Christian love: our (natural and innocent, but merely natural, not heavenly) pleasure in *being loved*—in being, as you say, an object of interest to someone—can be mistaken for progress in love itself, the outgoing active love which is concerned with giving, not receiving. It is this latter which is the beginning of sanctity.

But of course you know all this: alas, so much easier to know in theory than to submit to day by day in practice! Be very regular in your prayers and communions: and don't value special "guidances" any more than what comes thro' ordinary Christian teaching, conscience, and prudence.

I am shocked to hear that your friends think of following *me*. I wanted them to follow Christ. But they'll get over this confusion soon, I trust.

Please accept my deepest sympathy.

(CL 3, 500–501)

Our best havings are wantings

TO DOM BEDE GRIFFITHS   NOVEMBER 5, 1954

About death, I go through different moods, but the times when I can *desire* it are never, I think, those when this world seems harshest. On the contrary, it is just when there seems to be most of Heaven already here that I come nearest to longing for the *patria* [homeland]. It is the bright frontispiece [which] whets one to read the story itself. All joy (as distinct from mere pleasure, still more amusement) emphasizes our pilgrim status: always reminds, beckons, awakes desire. Our best havings are wantings.

(CL 3, 522–523)

To a correspondent who was having to put her pet down

TO MARY WILLIS SHELBURNE   AUGUST 18, 1956

I will never laugh at anyone for grieving over a loved beast. I think God wants us to love Him *more*, not to love creatures (even animals) *less*. We love everything *in one way* too much (i.e. at the expense of our love for Him) but in another way we love everything too little.

No person, animal, flower, or even pebble, has ever been loved too much—i.e. more than every one of God's works deserves. But you need not feel "like a murderer." Rather rejoice that God's law allows you to extend to Fanda that last mercy which (no doubt, quite rightly) we are forbidden to extend to suffering humans. You'll get over this.

(CL 3, 782)

C. S. LEWIS

On aging bodies as old cars

TO MARY WILLIS SHELBURNE   SEPTEMBER 30, 1958

I also have been in the hands of the dentist but much less unpleasantly than you; I know a "dry socket" after an extraction can be the very devil and all. We must both, I'm afraid, recognize that, as we grow older, we become like old cars—more and more repairs and replacements are necessary. We must just look forward to the fine new machines (latest Resurrection model) which are waiting for us, we hope, in the Divine garage!

(CL 3, 975)

On lilies and wrinkles

TO MARY WILLIS SHELBURNE   OCTOBER 30, 1958

I suppose living from day to day ("take no thought for the morrow") is precisely what we have to learn—though the Old Adam in me sometimes murmurs that if God wanted me to live like the lilies of the field, I wonder why He didn't give me the same lack of nerves and imagination as they enjoy! Or is that just the point, the precise purpose of this Divine paradox and audacity called Man—to do *with* a mind what other organisms do without it?

As for wrinkles—pshaw! Why shouldn't we have wrinkles? Honorable insignia of long service in this warfare.

(CL 3, 984–985)

To a friend whose wife had just died

TO SIR HENRY WILLINK DECEMBER 3, 1959

I have learned now that while those who speak about one's miseries usually hurt one, those who keep silence hurt more. They help to increase the sense of *general* isolation which makes a sort of fringe to the sorrow itself. You know what cogent reason I have to feel *with* you: but I can feel *for* you too. I know that what you are facing must be worse than what I must shortly face myself, because your happiness has lasted so much longer and is therefore so much more intertwined with your whole life. As Scott said in like case "What am I to do with that daily portion of my thoughts which has for so many years been hers?"

People talk as if grief were just a feeling—as if it weren't the continually renewed shock of setting out again and again on familiar roads and being brought up short by the grim frontier post that now blocks them. I, to be sure, believe there is something beyond it: but the moment one tries to use that as a consolation (that is not its function) the belief crumbles.

It is quite useless knocking at the door of Heaven for earthly comfort: it's not the sort of comfort they supply there.

You are probably very exhausted physically. Hug that and all the little indulgences to which it entitles you. I think it is tiny little things which (next to the very greatest things) help most at such a time.

I have myself twice known, after a loss, a strange excited (but utterly un-spooky) sense of the person's presence all about me. It may be a pure hallucination. But the fact that it always goes off after a few weeks proves nothing either way.

I wish I had known your wife better. But she has a bright place in my memory.

(CL 3, 1102)

An illusion caused by sorrow

TO PHOEBE HESKETH   JUNE 14, 1960

The most mischievous—and painful—by-product of any sorrow is the illusion that it isolates one, that one is kicked out alone for this from an otherwise cheerful, bustling, "normal" world. How much better to realize that one is just doing one's turn in the line like all the rest of the ragged and tired human regiment!

(CL 3, 1162)

To a correspondent who had been diagnosed with a "dangerous" disease

TO MARY WILLIS SHELBURNE   MARCH 19, 1963

I'm sorry they threaten you with a painful disease. "Dangerous" matters much less, doesn't it? What have you and I got to do but make our exit? When they told me I was in danger several months ago, I don't remember feeling distressed.

I am talking, of course, about *dying*, not about *being killed*. If shells started falling about this house I should feel quite differently. An external, visible, and (still worse) audible threat at once wakes the instinct of self-preservation into fierce activity. I don't think natural death has any similar terrors.

(CL 3, 1415)

On perseverance and its reward

TO MRS. JOHNSON   MARCH 13, 1956

Keep on, keep on: "To him that overcometh I will give the Morning Star."* All blessings.

*Revelation 2:26–28

(CL 3, 720)

C. S. LEWIS

On facing a possibly terminal illness

TO MARY WILLIS SHELBURNE   JUNE 17, 1963

Pain is terrible, but surely you need not have fear as well? Can you not see death as the friend and deliverer? It means stripping off that body which is tormenting you: like taking off a hair-shirt or getting out of a dungeon. What is there to be afraid of? You have long attempted (and none of us does more) a Christian life. Your sins are confessed and absolved. Has this world been so kind to you that you should leave it with regret? There are better things ahead than any we leave behind.

Remember, tho' we struggle against things because we are afraid of them, it is often the other way round—we get afraid *because* we struggle. Are you struggling, resisting? Don't you think Our Lord says to you "Peace, child, peace. Relax. Let go. Underneath are the everlasting arms. Let go, I will catch you. Do you trust me so little?"

Of course this may not be the end. Then make it a good rehearsal.

Yours (and like you a tired traveler, near the journey's end)*

*Lewis died about five months after this letter was written. The correspondent lived another twelve years.

(CL 3, 1430–1431)

Coping with physical and mental decline

TO MARY WILLIS SHELBURNE   JUNE 28, 1963

I think the best way to cope with the mental debility and total inertia is to submit to it entirely. Don't *try* to concentrate. Pretend you are a dormouse or even a turnip.

But of course I know the acceptance of inertia is much easier for men than for women. We are the lazy sex. Think of yourself just as a seed patiently waiting in the earth; waiting to come up a flower in the Gardener's good time, up into the *real* world, the real waking. I suppose that our whole present life, looked back on from there, will seem only a drowsy half-waking. We are here in the land of dreams. But cock-crow is coming. It is nearer now than when I began this letter.

(CL 3, 1434)

The "solemn fun" of nearing the end

TO SISTER PENELOPE   SEPTEMBER 17, 1963

I was unexpectedly revived from a long coma—and perhaps the almost continuous prayers of my friends did it—but it would have been a luxuriously easy passage and one almost (but *nella sua voluntade e nostra pace**) regrets having the door shut in one's face. Ought we to honor Lazarus rather than Stephen as the protomartyr? To be brought back and have all one's dying to do *again* was rather hard.

If you die first, and if "prison visiting" is allowed, come down and look me up in Purgatory.

It *is* all rather fun—solemn fun—isn't it?**

*"in His will is our peace"

**C. S. Lewis died the following month, on November 22, 1963.

ABOUT C. S. LEWIS

CLIVE STAPLES LEWIS (1898–1963) WAS ONE OF THE intellectual giants of the twentieth century and arguably one of the most influential writers of his day. He was a Fellow and Tutor in English Literature at Oxford University until 1954, when he was unanimously elected to the Chair of Medieval and Renaissance Literature at Cambridge University, a position he held until his retirement. He wrote more than thirty books, allowing him to reach a vast audience, and his works continue to attract thousands of new readers every year. His most distinguished and popular accomplishments include *Out of the Silent Planet*, *The Great Divorce*, *The Screwtape Letters*, and the universally acknowledged classics in The Chronicles of Narnia series. To date, the Narnia books have sold over 100 million copies and have been transformed into three major motion pictures.

ABOUT THE EDITOR AT LARGE

DAVID C. DOWNING IS THE FORMER R. W. SCHLOSSER Professor of English at Elizabethtown College and the Marion E. Wade Professor of Christian Thought at Wheaton College.

Downing grew up in Colorado, graduated from Westmont College in Santa Barbara, and earned his MA and PhD from UCLA.

Downing has written four scholarly books on C. S. Lewis: *Planets in Peril* (1992), a critical study of the Ransom trilogy; *The Most Reluctant Convert* (2002), an examination of Lewis's journey to faith; *Into the Wardrobe* (2005), an in-depth overview of the *Narnia Chronicles*; and *Into the Region of Awe* (2005), a study of how Lewis's wide reading in Christian mysticism enhanced his own faith and enriched his imaginative writing. Downing also provided a critical introduction and over four hundred explanatory notes to the new edition of C. S. Lewis's *The Pilgrim's Regress,* originally published in 1933 and reissued by Eerdmans in the Wade Center Annotated Edition (2014).

Downing previously edited two collections of excerpts from C. S. Lewis: *The Reading Life* and *C. S. Lewis on Writing (and Writers)*.

Downing currently resides in Boulder, Colorado, with his wife, Crystal, who is also an English professor and a published author.